INDEX

INDEX ON CENSORSHIP 4 1998

WEBSITE NEWS UPDATED EVERY TWO WEEKS
www.indexoncensorship.org
contact@indexoncensorship.org
tel: 0171-278 2313
fax: 0171-278 1878

Volume 27 No 4 July/August 1998 Issue 183

Index on Censorship (ISSN 0306-4220) is published bi-monthly by a non-profit-making company: Writers & Scholars International Ltd, Lancaster House, 33 Islington High Street, London N1 9LH. *Index on Censorship* is associated with Writers & Scholars Educational Trust, registered charity number 325003

Periodicals postage: (US subscribers only) paid at Newark, New Jersey. Postmaster: send US address changes to *Index on Censorship* c/o Mercury Airfreight International Ltd Inc, 365 Blair Road, Avenel, NJ 07001, USA

© This selection Writers & Scholars International Ltd, London 1998
© Contributors to this issue, except where otherwise indicated

EDITORIAL

Change and renewal

There is nothing monolithic about Gypsy (or Roma) culture – it is multi-voiced and fragmented. Too often their history, literature and mythology are recorded and interpreted by outsiders. In this issue of Index we emphasise the Roma's own writings – so central to modern Gypsy identity – their voices reclaiming and recalling personal and communal stories in fiction, poetry and autobiography. The Roma are fighting for their survival, as Ian Hancock says, 'not with the sword but with the pen.'

Living scattered all over Europe, the Roma are a minority that does not conveniently fit either national or linguistic definitions. Their world is, for the most part, a hidden one, ignored, unknown – and persecuted. The devastating Nazi persecution of Gypsies followed centuries of historical precedent set by virtually every country in Europe. Today, the Roma are still relentlessly discriminated against and marginalised, facing intensifying racial hatred and violence. Ironically, they are the one ethnic people who have tried to live with ecological and community values for centuries and yet have been treated with contempt for it, forced from rural life into urban shanty towns, from traditional crafts into menial jobs and unemployment – which in turn has led to conflict with local communities. They are in fact the pariahs of Europe.

But things are changing. As this file reflects, a new generation of Rom intellectuals and activists in Europe are forming organisations, demanding recognition and cultural autonomy, setting up broadcasts on radio and TV, establishing museums of Gypsy life. This Gypsy activism, sometimes riven with internal differences, attempts to link political and cultural awareness, refuses dependency and victimhood, and is making public the case of Europe's largest and most despised minority.

We publish our file on Iran's press one year into the new government of President Khatami, and with the *fatwa* on Salman Rushdie still not lifted. Indeed, there are signs as we go to press that the (minority) government is losing some battles against the old fundamentalist guard. But this year has, nevertheless, seen a remarkable opening up of debate and free expression, not simply in the press but in Iran's cultural life, especially among the younger generation. Public libraries are being restocked with once forbidden books, films that have gathered dust on the censors' shelves are being distributed. We welcome this change and will keep our readers posted. ❏

contents

On the Romany trail

Football and ferment in Iran

LETTERS

Benetton anger

From Anne Harrison,
Canada

I was shocked and angered to
see this ad (*below*) in my issue
of Index. Benetton was one of
the first to bring back the
practice of 'piece work' – a
practice which guarantees lower
wages, more work for less money,
very little
protection against
unemployment,
work-related
accidents etc. It's
a terrible practice
that should have
been left in the
last century. If
Benetton has
reformed their
ways since then –
my apologies to
them. But not to
you – Benetton
sells clothes, not
freedom – how
can I take your
magazine
seriously now?
Just cancel my
subscription
please. I don't
want any more
bullshit. ❑

Justice and change

Cynthia Kee,
London

In his article about the hollow
ring of Israel Independence
celebrations in the US (*Fifty years
of dispossession; Index 3/98*),
Edward Said bangs on about the
hideous inequities rampant in that
country today – inequities of

EVERYONE
HAS THE RIGHT
TO FREEDOM
OF OPINION
AND EXPRESSION
(art.19)

FIFTIETH ANNIVERSARY
OF THE UNIVERSAL
DECLARATION
OF HUMAN RIGHTS

UNITED COLORS
OF BENETTON.

mindblowing stupidity and shortsightedness. He does it with eloquence and elegance presenting an arid catalogue of such abuse and denial, papered over with international agreements and handshakes on the White House lawn, that explosion seems the only tolerable option in the face of such an accumulation of mutual fear, hate and repression.

And yet, embedded in the text is a passing reference to 'Adalah (the Arab word for justice) an Arab-Jewish organisation within Israel.'

Professor Said, there are hundreds of projects, programmes, initiatives, organisations run by Israelis themselves – both Arab and Jewish – devoted to conciliation, co-existence, co-education. They operate at every level from local (B'Tselem: the Israel Information Centre for Human Rights in the Occupied Territories) to national (the Movement for Quality Government); from A (Adam Institute for Democracy and Peace) to W (Workers' Hotline). Among the dozen or so I personally have visited, there's: Neve Shalom/Wahat-al-Salem, the peace village where Arabs and Jews live together and are educated side by side; the Jewish

Arab Association for the Child and family in Jaffa...

I suggest that it is these ventures that need attention; these exercises in resolution that deserve support; this painstaking process of humanisation of stereotypes that requires encouragement – not endorsement of the status quo. Confrontation and violence are the most primitive ways of defusing frustration.

I think Professor Said could have made his point just as well by calling attention to these unofficial experiments in peace and, thereby, given his endorsement to the possibility of change. ❑

● **After-taste** The UK's Broadcasting Standards Commission condemned an episode of Channel 4's *TV Dinners* in late May, ruling that the 'norms' of cookery programming had been broken 'in a way which would have been disagreeable to many'. But Channel 4 defended presenter Rosie Clear for preparing a 'perfectly healthy dish with a centuries-old tradition'. The sight of her own placenta being sautéed with garlic and butter and then ground into a paté and served to guests was too much for nine viewers to digest. The Independent Television Commission, however, upheld Clear's recipe which, it said, did not breach its code on 'taste'.

● **Your campaign has been disconnected** Mobile telephone manufacturer Nokia stopped a huge poster campaign in Germany in June after discovering that its advertising slogan *Jedem das Seine* (To each his own) was the same as the motto over the gates of Buchenwald concentration camp. The Finnish company was forced to remove 3,000 posters and pulp thousands of brochures following protests from the Berlin branch of the American-Jewish Congress.

● **Into the storm** On the eve of President Clinton's visit to China, the first since the 1989 Tiananmen Square massacre, Beijing assumed a pugnacious stance by revoking the entry visas issued at the White House to three journalists from Radio Free Asia (RFA), a station it has often jammed in the past. RFA enjoys the support of the President and of Congress; the latter trebled its funding last September to ensure round-the-clock broadcasts to Tibet and Xinjiang, as well as to boost existing services in Mandarin and Cantonese (*Index* 6/1997). In anticipation of the visit, the Chinese authorities locked up several dissidents in cities along the route of the presidential itinerary.

● **Aria diplomacy** A plan to open the Lincoln Centre's prestigious Festival '98 in New York with a rare performance of the *Peony Pavilion*, a 20-hour opera based on a 400-year-old Chinese love story, was aborted after censors in Shanghai impounded the sets and refused to let the cast leave the country. In clear counterpoint to Bill Clinton's embarrassing introit to Beijing, officials called the opera 'feudal, superstitious and pornographic', insisting that it be 'extensively revised' before going on tour. After New York, the Kunqu Opera company was to have performed the *Peony Pavilion* in Paris, Caen, Sydney and Hong Kong.

● **Smoke – without fire** The *New York Times* reported in June a dinner conversation between an eye doctor and an Italian friend who was visiting the city after a long absence. He mentioned how impressed he was by Mayor Rudi Giuliani's clean-up campaign, but said he was equally saddened by the apparent increase in prostitution. When questioned as to how he had come to that conclusion, the man replied that everywhere he went there were well-dressed women idling in doorways smoking. The eye doctor had to explain that this was merely a result of the city's stern anti-smoking policy.

● **Middlesex and the market** The 25-year-old in-house magazine of Middlesex University, *North Circular*, gained an enviable reputation for adventurous reporting under editors Ray Rickett and Bobby di Joia. But times have changed. On 2 April, its most recent editor, Suzi Clark, a widow with two children, was told to clear her desk after 'allegations' that 'were too serious to be divulged to her' but that 'would not be investigated further' if she moved to a less sensitive post. Her crime was to contemplate publishing an article by philosophy professor Jonathan Rée, in which he described a market-led shift toward a 'culture of fearful conformity, a regime of top-down Middlesex-mindedness'. *Quod erat demonstrandum.*

● **Stumped!** By late May the nuclear test match between India and Pakistan was very hard to score. On 28 May, the country's official media reported that the nation had exploded two nuclear devices, then Prime Minister Nawaz Sharif said on TV that the number of tests had been five. Two days later, Foreign Minister Gohar Ayub Khan announced that two more tests had taken place that day, while Foreign Secretary Shamshad Ahmed told a press conference that there had only been one. For confused spectators, the bigger question was who on earth was umpiring the nuclear team.

● **Tall storey** A Tennessee bookstore avoided obscenity charges on 8 June by agreeing to place three books on shelves at least five-and-a-half feet above the floor. The three books – photographer Jock Sturgis' *Radiant Identities* and *The Last Day of Summer* and David Hamilton's *Age of Innocence* – contain photographs of nude children. The Barnes & Noble bookstore in Franklin was indicted in November 1997 for violating a state law that says 'questionable material' must be kept out of the reach of children. A Barnes & Noble store in Nashville has a similar case pending.

● **Service with a smile** A delegation of the Turkish Human Rights Commission visiting prisons and police stations in south-east Turkey said it was astonished at security force attitudes on finding clubs and lorry tyres locked in interrogation centre storerooms. When the group found a small gadget used to dispense electric current and asked what it was, police said they used it 'to listen to those being interrogated'. On interrogation techniques, one officer said: 'We sit here at the table and ask in a manner, respectful of human rights, whether the person has committed a crime.' His colleague added: 'Interrogation is a very enjoyable job.'

● **Lawyer's lament** Maricopa County Sheriff Joe Arpaio wants to ban *A Son Gone Too Soon*, a song written by the father of a man who died in Arpaio's Arizona jail in November 1996, and who is now suing the Sheriff for US$20 million. Arpaio says the song is an attempt to 'poison' his reputation in advance of jury selection for the damages action'. He wants the court to stop Jaron Norberg reciting the song he wrote, or even talking about it in public.

● **Silent voices** When the gay paper *Southern Voice* in Atlanta, Georgia switched to the Gainesville printer of *The Atlanta Times* in early May, it was to take advantage of lower costs. The owners didn't realise it would be their last deadline. Two local ministers circulated pamphlets condemning the new deal. 'Contact *The Times*' advertisers ... and tell them of your dissatisfaction,' spluttered one. Then, in the first week of June, the *Southern Voice* fell silent. *The Times* said the printing had stopped because of problems that were 'purely operational.'

● **Crazy name, crazy guy**

Anyone familiar with Israel's moral guardians would not have been surprised by their response when transsexual 'love ambassador' Dana International represented their country in the Eurovision Song Contest and was crowned Queen of the Carnival of Kitsch. But who can fathom the logic of this outburst from Egyptian writer Mohammed al-Ghitti? 'They have fabricated a Jewish prostitute and called her Dana International for her to send her moans and disgraceful words from the City of a Thousand Minarets to invade all Arab cities and impose her crazy artistry on people's taste.' Everyone defines the boundaries of his/her own taste, but for the toast of Europe they seemed to stop short of the Spice Girls. The diva reportedly rejected an offer in June to replace the departed Geri Halliwell in the five-girl line-up.

Rupert Clayton

● **King of comedy**

You have to hand it to President Lukashenka, the *Ubu Roi* of Belarus. Mid-June's 'battle of the residences', in which Minsk embassies were told to vacate their premises so that the 'plumbing could be fixed', triggered a diplomatic incident not just with one foreign power, but an Olympic-standard 22. Foreign Minister Ivan Antanovich had said on 9 June that the Drozdy diplomatic compound would wind up 'floating in its own sewage', if the embassies were not vacated, but the ambassadors feared that a different kind of 'plumbing' would be installed during their absence. By the end of June, at least 7seven countries had broken off relations with Minsk, citing its violation of the Vienna Convention on diplomatic protocol which classifies ambassadors' residences as foreign territory.

True to form, the outcry was totally incomprehensible to its architect. Why did the ambassadors object, he asked rhetorically, to his declaring the compound part of his own presidential residency. After all, they would have the honour of residing there as his guests. To object to such small 'inconveniences' as moving out temporarily, or to carrying new security passes was, his spokesman said, absolutely unreasonable. It was the ambassadors, not the President, who had breached the protocols.

In today's Belarus, there are no limits on the bizarre. On 19 June – the Day of the Great Lock-out – the presidential security force barred diplomatic cars from the Drozdy compound, but allowed the French ambassador to enter on a motorbike, since that form of transport had not been prohibited in their instructions.

And with Minsk's own ambassadors summarily sent home with messages of disapproval, the remaining embassy staff were faced with the unenviable task of hosting receptions on 3 July, the anniversary of the restoration of Soviet rule in 1944. In his own brand of 'newspeak', Lukashenka has decreed this to be Belarus' new independence day. On the bright side, it was unlikely there would be much washing up to do.

Vera Rich

● **Deconstructing Beck**

An alliance of artists and cultural saboteurs avoided an extended legal battle recently when lawyers for California musician Beck backed down on a suit against a CD called *Deconstructing Beck*. Or so it would seem. The CD, created by copyright activists Illegal Art and produced with money from culture sabotage group RTMark, took songs written by Beck, sliced and diced them, and re-ordered the pieces at random to make a statement about copyright law and sampling in today's music industry.

Beck's record company, Geffen, was at the top of the list when it came to promoting the CD, and legal letters began flying in all directions with the words 'cease and desist' usually front and centre. Then, late in May, the letters stopped flowing and the

rumours began pouring in. Sources report the rumour that Beck had asked lawyers at Geffen to stop the legal action, but that he refuses to admit this because he doesn't like the CD. Beck's publicist has refused the chance to comment, but others have not. 'Why should it matter what he thinks of it, if he agrees with the issues raised?' asked a spokesperson for RTMark.

Since the issue is the clearance of copyright on samples of other artists' work, some say Beck would be hard-pressed to prove that he gets clearance for all the samples he uses in his own music. But before things got that far, someone at Geffen forwarded a letter to RTMark from the Advisory on Law Practice in Art. The letter plainly described the trouble Geffen would have if it tried to prosecute over *Deconstructing Beck*. So now everyone, except possibly Beck, is happy.

'A court case only helps us if we win but, if we don't go to court, that helps establish the viability of common law', Philo T Farnsworth, the pseudonymous force behind Illegal Art, said on 14 June. 'Maybe it is better if we hope for more of an understanding between artists that sampling isn't stealing if it is used to create a new work.'

Andrew Elkin

VERAN MATIC

Terms of estrangement

Media control has always been vital to rallying domestic support for Serbian aggression in the Balkans. As Kosovo follows Bosnia into outright war, a less bloody but still critical battle is taking place over language – and the uses to which it is put.

Kosovo has always belonged to the Serbs and it will stay that way. This is the invariable assertion of Serb and Yugoslav politicians. The more the international community insists that the borders must not change, that Kosovo's independence is impossible, the more Serb negotiators repeat this article of faith. The religious-minded public often terms Kosovo the 'Sacred Land': Kosovo is Jerusalem – with Serbs implicitly compared with the Jews. Both sides in the Kosovo debate appeal to history, culture, religion and demography, but the thrust of their arguments is couched in linguistics.

The media are directly involved in the formulation of this debate and differences between them are quickly identified in their use of language and terminology. The state-controlled – especially the electronic – media refer to the province by the word *Metohija*, the western part that borders Montenegro and Albania and is the location of the greatest number of Serbian monasteries. Since before World War II, the term *Kosmet* had taken root, though it is used only by Serbs. In all legal descriptions, *Kosovo* is the home of *Kosovo Albanians*. But the state media today use the term *shiptar* almost exclusively to refer to Kosovo Albanians.

Although derived from *Shqiptar* – the word used by Albanians to describe themselves – the Serbian variant is wholly pejorative. Its adoption by the state media coincided with the escalation of the conflict in Kosovo. It had all but vanished from sight after the Dayton Agreement, when President Slobodan Milosevic made a U-turn towards peace. But terminology is an inherent part of war and daily politics. Yugoslavia's much-reduced independent media, both print and electronic, continue to use the terms *Kosovo* and *Kosovo Albanians*.

Another terminological shift occured with the outbreak of the repressive operations in Kosovo in February 1998. This brought the terms *shiptar terrorists, shiptar gangs* and the softer *shiptar secessionists* into favour. The term *balist* is used in state media to refer to the pro-Fascist Kosovo Albanian troops who collaborated with Germans and Italians during World War II. State bodies, particularly the Serbian police, are most typically described as the *forces of order*.

The first open clash between the regime and the independent media over reports from Kosovo concerned terminology. After the Drenica massacre in March, when the independent media reported that so many *Albanians* – rather than *terrorists* – had perished, the deputy public prosecutor tabled procedures against them for 'campaigning against the state', while the state-controlled media launched their more serious campaign against Albanians. One reason for such a reaction was the refusal of the independents to restrict themselves to one source of information only – the official source.

Analysis of the comparative coverage of Kosovo by the state and independent media provides one clue to the regime's sensitivity to terminological and semantic liberty. Between February and May, when the gravest clashes occured, with casualties on both sides, the state media reported in a minimalist manner. Headlines such as 'Terrorist Hideout Destroyed' pushed aside any data on civilian casualties, the scale of the operation, the impact on civilian facilities or the strength of the forces engaged.

The independents concentrated on reports from the conflict zones. This news occupied their front pages and prime time broadcasts, providing details of casualties, civilian victims, the kinds of injuries sustained, missing persons, the destruction of property, the disruption of traffic and other humanitarian considerations. Such information occupied some 40 per cent of news volume, blunting the edge of the state media's war-mongering. On *Radio B92*, an average of 15 minutes of every 24-minute news programme concerned Kosovo, more than half the total news coverage. Magazine programmes such as 'Focus' dedicate at least one, and often three, of its five sections to Kosovo.

One direct result of this style of reporting was the dismal response to the call-up notices to army and police reserves. But the regime responded to the mass refusal to fight in Kosovo with fresh attacks on the *enemy within* and the *traitors* gathered around the independent media. The war in Kosovo rapidly turned into a showdown with the *unpatriotic* section of Serbia's population.

In the second phase of the Kosovo crisis, a referendum was held to determine whether foreign mediators should be permitted to negotiate the future status of the province. The issue occupied nearly half the available space in the state media, then bent on an intensive referendum campaign. The first meeting between Kosovo Albanian leader Ibrahim Rugova and Milosevic, that marked the beginning of the third phase in the Kosovo dynamic, received only moderate coverage from the state information apparatus: the independents covered the event exhaustively. A similar division can be seen in the most recent, and openly violent phase. State media continually refer to members of the Albanian opposition as *shiptar terrorists*, while the independent media now call them *members of the Kosovo Liberation Army*.

The tendency of the state media to suppress information about the scale of clashes, their territorial scope and possible impact upon civilians is by now transparent. Filtering is applied, in particular, to details about the Yugoslav Army, the conditions of recruits and their quality of training and equipment. That large numbers of police reserves refused to answer the call to go to Kosovo — a story revealed only by the independents — highlights the fact that it is neither the police nor the army that is the regime's most loyal ally, but the state media.

There was a joke in Belgrade a couple of years ago that, if Germany had had an editor from Serbian state television instead of Goebbels, the public would never have learned that they had lost the war. This is abundantly true of Kosovo. ❏

Veran Matic *is editor-in-chief of Belgrade's Radio B92 and chairman of the Association of Independent Economic Media. Translated by Marija Milosavljevic.*

DRAZEN PANTIC

Web wars

The conflict in Kosovo is unique: it is the first small war to grasp the propaganda possibilities of the Net. But giving Kosovans their own voice is not easy

The effort to establish internet links in Kosovo and network as many people as possible – regardless of ethnicity – dates back to the launch of independent internet centres in Serbia. OpenNet, the country's first provider, has been working to expand Kosovo's links and ensure their permanence.

Over the past two-and-a-half years, a large number of Kosovans have attended OpenNet classrooms. Among them were independent student groups and priests of the Serbian Orthodox Church. Father Sava, a peace activist from the Decani monastery, took his first steps on the internet in an OpenNet classroom.

The effort to get Kosovo linked to the internet included a project to establish the link via a telephone line permanently leased to the independent Kosovo Albanian daily *Koha Ditore*. The equipment and infrastructure have been paid for but *Telekom Srbije* has still failed to install the line, claiming 'technical problems'. The project includes the establishment of an internet classroom in Pristina, which would offer access for all, without discrimination.

In the absence of the permanent line, a large number of independent journalists in Kosovo, primarily those from *Koha*, have been given access to servers in Belgrade. A permanent and uncensored e-mail exchange has also been established. The news produced by the paper is then re-broadcast on the internet by OpenNet's servers.

The reaction of the internet public to support for the independent media in Kosovo has been curious. During the wars in former Yugoslavia, Serbian web-users generally kept their distance from the state media. Early this year, however, when the crisis in Kosovo escalated, the normally-peaceable browsers seemed to perceive every news item, every hot link to any Kosovan medium as an act of open treason.

As a result, OpenNet has received a large number of threatening e-mail messages, worded as never before, due to the links we established with the *Koha* web site. The fiercest reactions came after OpenNet put all *Radio B92* documentaries about Kosovo on the Net. Most reactions were intemperate, ranging from wild approval to threats. Oddly enough, however, the most moderate reaction came from Serbians whose background was in Kosovo.

The fast and free flow of information, together with the need for direct and objective reporting from Kosovo, have led us to consider an even more intensive use of new technologies. We are now implementing a project that will enable independent journalist, students and other groups to send reports, including pictures and short documentaries, from Kosovo using DVD (Digital Vidoe Discs) cameras, mobile laptops and satellite telephones. ❏

Drazen Pantic is director of Radio B92's OpenNet, Serbia's first independent Internet provider.

KOHA DITORE, or *Arta Press*, posts daily updates in Albanian and English at **www.kohanet.com**. The same page includes a link to *Kosovo Online*, a service launched jointly with the Beta news agency in Belgrade. Texts are published in Albanian, Serbian and English. *Radio B92's* web pages, **www.siicom.com/odrazb** (Serbian) and **http://b92eng.opennet.org** (English), carry daily reports by *B92's* three Kosovo-based correspondents. Opennet's site **www.opennet.org** carries links to these web pages, as well as to the Real Audio stream of *B92's* programming. The website of the Stockholm-based *Kosova News* – **www.kosova.com** – provides a synopsis of articles from a pro-secessionist view. For the Yugoslav state's version of events, check **www.yugoslavia.com** or **www.kosovo.com/terror.html**

SIMON MARTIN

Air power

On 16 May the Serbian Telecommunications Ministry announced the results of its latest frequency tender, granting 247 temporary licences to radio and television stations. Some 425 stations applied but, of the 33 members of the Association of Independent Economic Media (ANEM), only *Radio B92* was granted a licence, albeit temporarily. Its Belgrade companion, *Radio Index*, was denied a licence, although it intended to continue broadcasting until shut down.

If allowed to resume broadcasting, the station will have to pay a 'user fee' of more than US$22,000 per month – despite a monthly budget of only US$10,000. Even *B92* will have difficulty finding the money, and there is no guarantee its licence will be renewed when it expires in one year's time. Only two other ANEM members, *TV Pancevo* and *F Kanal* were also awarded licences.

B92's editor-in-chief, Veran Matic, said the results indicated the regime's 'fear of independent and professional information'. He added that *B92* had been licenced solely to 'create the illusion of democracy at an international level'.

According to Matic, the ministry outlawed over 20 independent television stations, representing the giggest ban on electronic media in Europe's post-war history. All ANEM members decided to continue broadcasting despite the lack of licences and the association, together with several other media organisations and NGOs, lodged a complaint with the federal Constitutional Court on 26 May. ❏

Simon Martin

RICARDO UCEDA

Closure of the exposé factory

The Peruvian media and the government are in a state of virtual war

One of the most striking contradictions in Peru is the existence of a vibrant independent media, which attacks the régime of President Alberto Fujimori without restraint and continuously reports his government's efforts to stifle freedom of expression. The government, however, holds up this same energetic press as proof positive of its innocence, for it is logical that a muzzled media would not be so free to blast the president and his henchman Vladimiro Montesinos, unofficial head of the intelligence services, the anti-drug effort, the police force and part of the armed forces.

The clue to the puzzle is in the 1997 Report on Press and Democracy, prepared by the Instituto Prensa y Sociedad (IPYS). The report lists some 40 instances of violations against journalists during 1997. All are related to 'the precariousness of the Peruvian democratic system and, especially, to the role acquired by the armed forces and the intelligence services in the political life of the country'. IPYS defines the current situation of the press as 'semi-freedom in a semi-democracy'.

Ten months have elapsed since control of TV Channel 2 *Frecuencia Latina* passed from Israeli-born Baruch Ivcher, its majority shareholder, to Samuel and Mendel Winter, minority shareholders and now government allies, thanks to a judicial decision. Ivcher was deprived of his ownership rights because Channel 2 had turned into the government's most vociferous critic. How could a judge deprive someone of an inalienable right? The answer is simple: the judiciary has been under direct presidential control since 1992 when the president instigated a *coup d'état* and dismissed Congress.

The procedure used to deprive Ivcher of his media interests was a sophisticated operation to destroy the exposé factory which Channel 2 had become under his direction. On 6 April 1997 the station broadcast the testimony of a woman whose head was permanently tilted down because her neck could no longer support it. Leonor La Rosa, an Army Intelligence Services (SIE) agent, had been so savagely tortured by her 'comrades' that she is now entirely bed-ridden. On the same day, it was disclosed that another SIE operative, Mariella Barreto, had been beheaded and dismembered, presumably by her own colleagues.

On 13 April, an already shocked population was further astounded when *Frecuencia Latina* revealed that the all-powerful Vladimiro Montesinos, described by the government as a 'philanthropic collaborator' who 'did not charge a cent' for his advice, had declared a personal income during 1995 of more than US$50,000 per month. This was inconceivable for someone who supposedly spent his time between the General Army Headquarters and Government Palace and claimed to devote 18 hours a day to these activities.

What kind of services was Montesinos selling on the basis of the privileged information available to him ? Who – inside or outside the country – paid such splendid fees? The government experienced a wave of revulsion unmatched since the 1993 discovery of the remains of nine students and a professor from La Cantuta University, victims of the Colina death-squad. Mariella Barreto, wife of a member of Colina, was believed to have been executed for revealing where the victims had been buried. Reprisals against Ivcher for making such scandals public were not long in coming.

On 23 May the joint military command publicly accused Ivcher of fomenting a campaign aimed at 'harming the prestige and image of the armed forces'. Pro-military newspapers accused him of selling weapons to Ecuador, then at war with Peru. A judge charged Ivcher with contempt of court for not appearing as witness at an army trial. Government congressmen accused journalists at *Frecuencia Latina* with 'insulting' the armed forces because they had broadcast statements by Ecuadorian generals. Finally, on 10 June, the head of the National Police, General Dianderas, unveiled the *pièce de résistance* of the plot against Ivcher.

Visibly embarrassed, Dianderas disclosed that the dossier of Baruch Ivcher's naturalisation process 'did not exist'. Therefore, the owner of *Frecuencia Latina* was a foreigner and, under Peruvian law, was automatically disqualified from operating a TV channel. All that remained was to switch on the judicial machinery. Timely changes in the composition of the courts ensured that biased judges were appointed to hear Ivcher's testimony.

Evidence that the naturalisation dossier had, in fact, existed; the constitutionality of depriving a citizen of his nationality; proof of shameless manipulation: all Ivcher's arguments were dismissed outright. Instead, the courts upheld the claim of Samuel and Mendel Winter, the minority shareholders, who asked permission to take over the management of the TV channel in view of Ivcher's 'irregular situation'.

Nobody doubted that the orientation of *Frecuencia Latina* would change when, on 19 September, the Winters assumed control of the station. They had already made clear their disagreement with Ivcher's investigative style in personal visits to army generals. It was similarly public knowledge that the *Frecuencia Latina* investigative team would not continue under the new management. All resigned.

Ivcher sought refuge in Miami in June, to be followed in January 1998 by José Arrieta, former head of *Frecuencia Latina*'s investigative unit and the man responsible for the *Contrapunto* programme which had first broadcast La Rosa's testimony and the news of Barreto's assassination. Arrieta requested political asylum after deciding that returning home would be too dangerous. Police authorities and the anti-terrorism agency Dincote had already involved him in a bizarre investigation whose key character was an obscure SIE agent.

Late in 1995, SIE agent José Basan had visited Arrieta, then head of investigations at *América* Channel 4, offering to supply information on human rights violations for money. Arrieta said he would not pay and that any data that did emerge would need to be confirmed. Basan contacted other media, where his revelations were published throughout 1996. One year later, Basan accused Arrieta of conspiring against the army, saying that he had merely been following a script prepared by the journalist to smear officers. Far from being a penitent agent, Basan seems to have been explicitly briefed to gather information on the press and human rights organisations with which he had been in contact for several months.

Arrieta received his first summons to appear before Dincote on 15 December. He analysed the situation carefully. He had been under SIE surveillance since 1993 when, as a journalist with *Si* magazine, he was part of the team which revealed the truth about La Cantuta: that despite government denials, the killings had been committed by a squad run by SIE. He decided to accept an invitation to present his case in New York to the Committee to Protect Journalists.

To speak of physical danger is no exaggeration. Late in 1996, journalist Edmundo Cruz of the newspaper *La República*, published a well-documented report about the 'Bermuda' plan, prepared by SIE to harass the independent press. He further revealed the existence of an SIE operation to assassinate journalist Cesar Hildebrandt, host of *Frecuencia Latina*'s robust *En Persona* programme. The two schemes were later confirmed in the interviews with Leonor La Rosa and another SIE agent, Luisa Sanatta. By then, the SIE's dirty war against the media was an open secret. On 17 October 1996, police in Puno had arrested three SIE agents – Luis Barrantes, Favio Urquizo and Angel Sauni – after they successfully exploded two bombs at the offices of *Global* TV.

The capture of the bombers red-handed indicated, at the very least, the prospect of exemplary punishment. But disregarding even their own confessions of guilt, the judge acquitted the men. The outcome of other investigations linked to the press came as no surprise after that. Such as when, after a half-hearted inquiry, police concluded that 'common delinquents' had sequestered Blanca Rosales, chief editor of *La República*, for three hours on 1 April 1997; or when the men who brutally beat Luis Angeles Laynes, political editor of the independent paper *Ojo*, were never traced.

The polarisation of police and judiciary casts doubt on the effectiveness of any press-related inquiry, such as the murders of journalists Tito Pilco, director of Radio *Frecuencia Popular*, and Isabel Chumpitas and Jose Amaya, in Piura. Even when police do arrest those responsible, there is a lingering feeling that their intellectual authors are still at liberty.

Other independent reporters have become the victims of SIE campaigns of vilification. Editor Gustavo Mohme of *La República*, columnist Fernando Rospigliosi and investigator Edmundo Cruz were systematically reviled in the yellow press, but the attacks against Angel Paes, head of the investigation unit, exceeded all limits. For two months

– without missing a single day – the tabloid *El Tio* devoted a complete page to slurs on his professional and personal life. Frequently, the facing page carried a full-page ad from the Ministry of the Presidency.

No one considers suing, for there is no guarantee in Peru of a fair trial. Several reporters' phones were tapped by the national intelligence service SIN during the previous administration, according to revelations by *Frecuencia Latina*, which gave in evidence the unedited texts of bugged conversations. But the same judges who deprived Baruch Ivcher of his TV station refused even to grant the affected journalists an *Amparo* – Cease and Desist order – to prevent the phone-tapping continuing.

The independent media still harry the Fujimori administration, but no one knows who is listening in. Or when the next axe will fall. ❏

Ricardo Uceda, former editor-in-chief of Si *magazine, now edits* El Comercio *and is a member of the governing council of the media monitoring organisation,* Instituto Prensa y Sociedad.

ARNOLD KOHEN

Muffled voices

As Suharto tumbled, East Timor experienced a frisson of free speech – tempered by the fear of a return to the usual pogrom

On 4 June, the military commander of East Timor, his superior officer and a dozen other officers died in a helicopter crash. President Suharto had left office two weeks before on 21 May. It was eerily quiet along the coast road, normally crowded with foodstalls run by immigrants, the air thick with *kretik*, the clove-flavoured cigarette popular in Indonesia.

For all the ugliness since the Indonesian invasion in 1975, East Timor, a former Portuguese colony the size of the Netherlands, is still a land of breathtaking beauty, with incomparable mountain views and crystal springs, some of which tumble into Baucau, where Nobel Prize winner, Roman Catholic Bishop Carlos Ximenes Belo, grew up. Mountains rise a short distance from the Banda Sea, virtually up from the shore.

The island was separated culturally from the rest of the archipelago hundreds of years ago, and two decades of heavy-handed Indonesian rule have done nothing to narrow the gap. They have only confirmed East Timor's sense of nationalism, which went on rare display on 6 June. That day, a gathering of 'six or seven' local leaders was called at a hall behind the governor's palace to discuss the territory's future after the fall of President Suharto. Those six or seven were reliable veterans of what passed for the sanctioned politics of East Timor. There seemed little to fear – at least, that is what the authorities thought.

Then there came an outburst of muffled voices. 'This is the end and the beginning!' one man shouted. 'Troops out!' said another. For most of the 23 years since Indonesian troops imposed martial law, people could do little in opposition. Now, for the moment, there was a rash of liberty. One of the six or seven leaders had allegedly spread the word that anyone who wished to express their views should come to the hall: perhaps 3,000 to 4,000 materialised.

The former Indonesian-appointed governor who chaired the event told the audience that they shouldn't worry about the omnipresent spies, because they had 'lost their power now that Suharto is gone'. But a young woman had said at the time: 'The intelligence officers are everywhere. They disguise themselves as meatball vendors and so on.'

The hall was a sea of banners: 'Viva Independence!', 'We want a referendum!' and 'Free Xanana Gusmao!' (Xanana is the *nom de guerre* of resistance leader José Alexandre Gusmao). Along the nearby banyan-lined street, nearly seven years earlier, thousands of marchers had passed on their way to Santa Cruz cemetery with similar signs. They paid dearly for that defiance: more than 250 people were killed and many more wounded after troops opened fire on the gathering. On 6 June, a similar meeting was held which, for the first time in 23 years, did not end in beatings, jailings or deaths.

That is what Carlos Felipe Ximenes Belo, who shared the 1996 Nobel Peace Prize with resistance spokesman Jose Ramos Horta, has been pleading for over the past decade. The bishop had demanded a withdrawal of Indonesian troops, the freeing of all political prisoners and the people's right to determine their own future through democratic means. But he skipped the assembly, preferring to send his Vicar General, Father José Antonio da Costa.

Belo publicly contradicted the initial assertion by new President Bacharuddin Jusuf Habibie that the government's policy on East Timor should remain unchanged. Beyond that, he made no secret of his opinion that East Timor's political leaders needed to act responsibly. There was at least one hopeful sign: a committee had been formed after 6 June to carry forward the political process.

The week before, at a youth festival at the Church of St Anthony of Motael where the march to Santa Cruz began in late 1991, Bishop Belo had said: 'The reforms in Jakarta must also affect the young people of East Timor. On this occasion,' he said, turning to Indonesian officials present, 'I suggest you abandon your suspicions toward our youth.'

But the bishop remained wary. The armed forces had yielded to popular pressure in Jakarta, but there was no mandate for change in East Timor. The structures that supported the Suharto system were still in place. Suharto's son-in-law, the ruthless Major General Prabowo Subianto, had been removed from his position as head of Strategic Command – the 'army of the army' as it is known. But while marginalised for the moment, Prabowo could still stage a comeback in Indonesia's volatile military politics.

The newfound freedom of expression took astonishing turns. A student leader, Fernando Araujo, demanded Xanana's release: 'If Habibie won't release Xanana,' he declared, 'we will continue to fight and die for the independence of our country.' Araujo had only recently been released after spending six years in prison, partly for asking fellow students to contact Amnesty about the Santa Cruz massacre.

The next major action was on 10 June, when several hundred students staged a demonstration at the University of East Timor in Dili. At Belo's urging, they refrained from marching through the the city, which might have provoked military retaliation. Things remained quiet, though the banners minced few words: 'Pull the armed forces out of Dili, end the bloodshed and free Xanana Gusmao,' said one.

A further challenge came on 12 June as word spread that 1,500 East Timorese students at Javanese universities would converge on Jakarta to demand independence and freedom for Xanana and the other political prisoners. They had reportedly sold all their belongings to pay for transport and food for what looked to be a dangerous enterprise. More than 1,000 East Timorese entered the foreign ministry and demanded a meeting to push their campaign for self-determination. The presence of the students was too much for General Wiranto, commander of the armed forces and Suharto's former adjutant. Security forces moved to end the protest – even as 12 political prisoners were freed in Dili. Troops and baton-wielding police charged into the students, whacking them with rattan sticks, fists and boots, then forcing them into 14 waiting buses which took them away for interrogation. Human rights sources said two demonstrators sustained broken legs and one was stabbed with a bayonet. Two East Timorese women were knocked unconscious. 'It's only Suharto who is gone, not the régime,' said one human rights worker.

On 14 June, Bishop Belo shared his worries about the possibility of new clashes, as another demonstration was about to take place in Dili. In his Sunday sermon, before thousands of people, Belo said: 'I ask all East Timorese to keep calm and restrained. Please don't create things which can disturb peace among people.' Habibie's offer of 'special status', he said, could be a 'transitional phase', though he emphasised that 'I'd like to see first. Not only promises.' Thus far, the idea of special status has been rejected by students, independence leaders and many ordinary people.

'East Timor should be free now,' said a middle-aged woman, a vegetable trader in Dili. 'So much blood has been shed ... we are ready for independence. I've witnessed the repression by Indonesia since the invasion. They have tortured and killed East Timorese. We don't want other people to rule our land any more.'

After talks with Belo on 15 June, leaders said they would suspend the protests. 'It is not only the students who are organising,' Belo had cautioned, 'the other side is organising too.' He spoke of *buffos* – Portuguese for 'clowns' – the provocateurs, linked to General Prabowo, who have engineered so many violent incidents in the past.

Bishop Belo also met President Habibie in Jakarta in June, the first direct contact between them at this time. The outcome is unknown. ❏

Arnold Kohen's biography, From The Place of the Dead: The Epic Struggles of Bishop Carlos Ximenes Belo of East Timor*, will be published by St. Martin's Press (New York) in early 1999.*

ANDRAS BIRO

What future for the Roma? An outsider's view

'The Romani population occupies a peculiar position. Despite its distinctly visible ethnicity, it has no political entity and no territory of its own' (*Andrzej Mirga & Nicolae Gheorghe*)

The tumescent face of a corpse recently appeared on the screen during the daily show *Police News* on Hungarian TV. The commentator was asking viewers to help identify the dead man who had been fished out of the Danube. It was the face of a Rom. I asked myself: was the drowned man the victim of a fight among drunks or was he killed because of the colour of his skin?

Ten years ago, such a question would not have occurred to me: the racist motivation would have been far fetched. Today, stories of individual and mob violence, police brutality, job discrimination are all too common in the media. What has happened?

The fall of the Berlin Wall is seen as the main political event of the end of our century, bringing democracy and political freedom to the peoples of the ex-dictatorships. At the same time, it shattered their sense of material security, however mediocre. Economic restructuring in the countries of Central and Eastern Europe (CEE) meant massive unemployment with the worse burden falling on the Roma. As competition between the majority population and the Roma for low paid jobs grew, intolerance and aggression increased. The weak and vulnerable needed a scapegoat – the other, the foreigner, the coloured one – to punish for their misfortune.

During the memorable 40 years of 'socialism', the Roma of CEE, who had been sedentary for decades, if not for centuries, were integrated by force into the mainstream economy at the lowest level of skills and income. This was accompanied by a high degree of acculturation involving a radical change in livelihood and lifestyle: literacy increased; modern housing, social security and health care became a regular feature of everyday life. The guarantee of a regular monthly income, till then an unimaginable state of material security, was the most notable change and broke the habits and attitudes of centuries.

Credit: Rex

At the first signs of economic crisis, however, the Roma workforce was pushed back into unemployment and returned to their familiar state of marginalisation and exclusion. Only a tiny group of businessmen was able to take advantage of the new market economy.

The recent wave of migration to Canada and western Europe, especially among Roma from the Czech Republic and Slovakia seeking asylum from persecution, was no more than the visible manifestation of the state of affairs at home. Western governments, with no more than 0.01 per cent of Roma in their populations, treated this influx mainly as an immigration problem. In the East, where they form between five and 10 per cent of the population – three quarters of Europe's Roma – they are seen as a region-wide social problem. But when it comes to human rights, the difference between the old and new democracies is insignificant. In both societies stereotypes and prejudices, frequently spilling over into violence, dominate discourse on the Roma.

The Roma are present throughout Europe. They are its largest minority and, some say, the only truly European community. Although separated by different histories, dialects, degree of integration into the majority society and, at times, with considerable distance between groups, adversity at the hands of non-Roma society has given the Roma a sense of community and common identity. This 'negative identity' is balanced by the strength and solidarity within the extended family, the basic social unit. To speak of the Roma as a monolithic group or culture is absurd; yet the persistence of negative stereotypes, allied with the animosity and violence against them, makes it not only possible but necessary to consider them as a single ethnic unit, a visible minority.

Their common roots, culture and faith, shared memories of the Nazi genocide and persecutions and continuing exclusion developed in Roma leaders the idea of non-territorial nationhood as a way of constructing a common sense of identity and a framework for defending their rights. Ethno-nationalism, with all its pros and cons, appeared as a vehicle of cohesion, mobilisation and awareness-building among activists.

1989 presented Roma leaders in the Balkans and Central and Eastern Europe with the opportunity to start building their own civil organisations. Constitutions which had previously neglected ethnic identities were now rewritten to acknowledge the existence of national and ethnic minorities. This provided the legal framework for the birth of hundreds of organisations: Roma political parties appeared on the scene, MPs and even elected self-governments materialised. For the first time in history, Roma civil organisations appeared on the national stage as Roma publicly assumed their ethnic identity. There is still a long way to go, but activism is incomparably higher than ever before.

The main debate among leaders centres on what exactly 'nationhood' means in terms of institutions, legal framework and status for the Roma inside their host societies. Different approaches include:

● the 'civil rights first' approach argues for the improvement of human rights in society as a whole, enabling the Roma to take their place as citizens within the framework of a liberal, democratic state. This view predominates where Roma are long-term, sedentary residents and to a very considerable degree integrated into the host community.

Some, a majority, see this as assimilation under a new guise and espouse
● a 'minority rights first' approach. This takes two forms: one
argues that the Roma are one of the minorities of any given state and
and as such should benefit with others from the rights such status
confers. The other underlines the non-territoriality and unique
transnational character of the Roma compared to other national
minorities. It claims that the Roma need special European status,
recognition and protection. This view is particularly relevant to groups
who have migrated to western Europe relatively recently and in some
ways anticipates the future status of all citizens of the European Union.

Emerging as they are at a time of political and economic upheaval
throughout CEE, the Roma movement faces many problems. Despite
the many cultural and historical differences between the two, a
comparison with the 1960s Black civil rights movement in the USA is
not without interest. Educational grants to returning servicemen after
WWII enabled a strong Black professional and intellectual leadership to
emerge in post-war America. In addition, they had solid support among
liberal groups in the North and from the churches. The emerging
Roma movement benefits from neither of these.

The Roma elite was formed under dictatorships lacking any
democratic norms, while the tiny non-Roma democratic opposition, at
that time a good ally of the Roma, was quickly absorbed by the new
governments after 1989, and its support lost. Allies of the Roma
movement can be counted on the fingers of one hand. The
development of Roma civil society is further hampered by the dire state
of unemployment and widespread poverty of most Roma. Rather than
mobilising the community to fight against their lot, this breeds apathy
and resignation.

The majority of early Roma NGOs mobilised around culture,
education and and tradition; those promoting the priority of civil rights
and political participation followed. At the same time, income-
generating schemes to alleviate poverty began to emerge. It became
clear to activists and leaders that without decent living standards the
development of the community as a whole was impossible, just as well-
being without human rights was impracticable. New strategies
increasingly combined economic and civil objectives.

The future of the Roma will greatly depend on how deeply and at what pace the societies and economies of CEE are integrated into the process of globalisation. Will, for instance, the gap in the labour market widen as production and services require ever more sophisticated skills? What happens if the influence of right wing parties continues to grow and exclusion and violence take on more serious proportions? Is assimilation or integration the answer? How will unemployed urban Roma youth deal with its growing frustrations? Is the Los Angeles syndrome a real threat? What educational strategies are appropriate for Roma children at a time when employment opportunities are not only diminishing but changing in character? Is the revival of disappearing traditional Roma skills a practical option? What about family planning: can the Third World-like rate of demographic growth continue? And so on.

Rather than playing prophet, let me express a fear and a hope.

A pessimistic reading of events is premised on the degree of socio-political instability and continuing intolerance and violence evidenced in the countries of the region over the last decade. In Lom, Bulgaria, for instance, as a final act of protest after having been deprived for months of social security payments by the mayor's office, a group of Roma decided to immolate themselves by fire. Extreme acts of this kind, which for the moment are directed against themselves, may well turn into aggression against the *gadje*, not, so far, characteristic of Roma resistance. In the Czech Republic, a politician of the extreme right campaigning on racist, anti-Roma slogans, has already been attacked physically by Roma at one of his meetings.

The proliferation of similar acts in a region where ethnic identity has become an explosive charge is a real threat; and the consequences for the much-needed development of democratic practices and the rule of law incalculable.

The more positive outcome depends on giving the Roma the social and political role in society its numbers warrant: on making it a real negotiating partner in the decision-making process within a democratic state. This could take several directions:

● From the bottom up by the consolidation at grass roots level of Roma civil society through its organisations. They would become the legitimate and authentic representatives of the community in a dialogue with local, regional and national bodies. This will demand a huge effort on the part of the leaders, requiring them to adopt democratic methods of organisation, to acknowledge and deal sympathetically with diversity and disagreement within the community, to develop a serious internal dialogue. At the same time, this could lead to a better developed sense of identity as well as building a professional and intellectual leadership capable of representing the diverse interests of the community as a whole. A common strategy focusing concern on the main problem areas among all the Roma – poverty, human rights and education – could build consensus among present and future Roma activists.

● Change at the top is crucial. The governments in the region which have done anything for the Roma are few, and political parties show little interest in espousing their cause on the practical grounds that to solicit one Roma vote would cost them at least one among the majority population. But since the winds blowing from the West stress the importance of human rights and minority issues, governments feel they must, at least formally, go along with the Europe they hope to join. Transforming fine words into actions will demand pressure from below – the Roma civil rights movement – and from above – the European Union. Already there are a few in government who recognise that failing to deal with the civil rights violations against the Roma could jeopardise the whole democratisation process.

● A fundamental change in attitude to the Roma within the majority populations of the region is a long way off. The foundations and associations that express solidarity with the Roma and promote concrete projects are few; trade unions and churches, the most influential organisations, are insensitive; the media, with rare exceptions, daily reproduce the stereotypes and contribute to the continuing exclusion of the Roma. The few organisations that are active on behalf of the Roma are seen as eccentric or romantic.

It remains to be seen whether governments and others will come to see that the future of the Roma is intimately connected with the future of their own societies: that dealing with Roma grievances is a matter of self interest. ❑

Andras Biro is the president of the European Roma Rights Center in Budapest

MORIS FARHI

The Gypsy Bible

The brutal and relentless persecution of the Roma, unleashed soon after their arrival in Europe, has been one of the greatest crimes of history. Hopes that the 'enlightenment' that so strongly condemned the Nazi's genocidal policies would finally enable this peaceful people to take its rightful place in the family of women have proved tenuous. Today the persecution of the Roma continues; in Eastern Europe, particularly, its virulence generates fears of a new Holocaust.

Children of the Rainbow tells the story of Branko, a survivor of Auschwitz, who sets out to liberate his people and to fulfil their secret yearnings for reunification in their mysterious homeland. Romanestan.

And he comes to hear of the 'Gypsy Bible', the holy scripture that made the Roma a great people, but which, according to oral tradition, perished in the mire of time. A Bible miraculously reclaimed, by a seer, from the collective memory of the Roma as they stood before the crematoria of Auschwitz. A Bible hidden and awaiting discovery. A Bible that prophesies his leadership. A Bible that will regenerate his people. That will reunite them. That will lead them to Romanestan...

And Branko finds this Bible...

1. Here is the descent of Branko, the son of Rom, the son of O Del, who was sent to Earth to undo the wicked deeds of Adam and who engraved his heavenly spoor as a leopard does.

O Del begat Rom, Rom begat Branko, Branko begat Rom, Rom begat Branko; and thereafter every shoot named his son after his father.

From Branko, grandson of O Del, to Branko Manu of the Flood are forty generations; from the Flood to Branko Theophilus of the Crucifixion are another forty generations; from the Crucifixion to Branko Mithras and the Dispersion from India are yet another forty generations; and from the Dispersion from India to Branko, the Bear-Tamer, who rose from the ashes of Porajmos, are a further forty generations.

2. Now, this is the story of the Flood.

When Adam's brood laid waste the east, west, south and north, Branko Manu asked O Del to divide him into four entities so that he could engage with the quadriform villains.

And O Del said unto him: 'Worry not. I will send a deluge and cleanse the earth. Go, build yourself an ark. Embark into it, you and your household. And take with you one pair, male and female, of every living thing I have made so that Creation can continue.'

Now, Adam, having overheard O Del, sidled up to Branko Manu's wife, Furrina, a vain woman, and seduced her with precious stones.

And Branko Manu built his ark; and the rains came; and the animals began to board.

Adam took the guise of a rat; and Furrina, who had agreed to smuggle him into the ark, mixed a heady ale for Branko Manu.

And when the male and female rats entered the ark, Adam sneaked in behind them.

Beholding three rats, the inebriated Branko Manu laughed and fondled his wife. 'Furrina, my love, you have mixed a mighty brew. I am seeing treble.'

Forty months later, the rains stopped.

Thereafter, each day, Branko Manu walked the receding waters. And whenever he found patches of earth, he released vegetation, male and female, and creatures, male and female, who would thrive there.

And all the animals and plants began to multiply.

And when the globe greened and the ark came aground, Adam gnawed his way out.

Then, stealing the perfumes of this new earth, he enticed Furrina to raise seed with him.

3. This is how the Romanies acquired their skills.

Lilith sent unto Rom a maiden called Uma who glowed with the splendour of Heaven.

And Uma bore Rom three sons in one go.

Unable to tell them apart, Rom proposed to name them all Branko; but Uma, knowing how each boy took breast differently, kept the name Branko for the firstborn and renamed the others Amengo and Singan.

When it was time to appoint tutors, Amengo was entrusted to the shepherd David, *mahatma* of the sling, the psalm and domestic animals;

Singan was consigned to Mulciber, *mahatma* over fire, metals, wood and cloth; and Branko was sent to the centaur, Chiron, *mahatma* of ethics, sport, music and medicine, and the magus of tricksters.

Thus Amengo became the wise man of flocks, herds, farmyard animals, and of poets and bards; Singan achieved excellence over cloth, wood, metals and fire; Branko acquired the trickster's innocent mischief and became the scourge of sham, vice and tyranny.

And when the sap rose in the boys' *kars*, they became betrothed to the Graces, those sisters who dulcify the living, even the scorpion.

Amengo took Euphrosyne; Singan took Aglaia; Branko took Thalia.

And after O Del took Rom and Uma to His bosom, the people gathered around the brothers.

Farmers, shepherds, herdsmen, hunters, poets and bards took their tents to Amengo; wainwrights, smiths, carpenters, weavers and potters aligned their wagons behind Singan; healers, thinkers, dancers, musicians, acrobats and horsemen travelled with Branko.

And they enjoyed many seasons of honest sweat, laughter and happy couplings.

4. This is the story of Branko, the Fire-Bearer.

When O Del went to create other galaxies, Adam consorted with petty gods and appropriated the fire.

Now, as it is known, fire is sacred to mankind because it is O Del's favourite guise for manifesting His presence.

Moreover, fire wards off the evil eye, protects the living from the dead, and, when lit at gravesides, warms the spirits.

Fire charts existence; no one may blow on it, lest, by putting it out, he extinguishes life also.

Branko undertook to liberate the fire.

He commissioned a Singan brother to make him a large, but hollow, wooden horse.

When this object was carpentered, he hid in its belly and asked an Amengo brother to take it to Adam as a gift; but so that Adam would not be suspicious of the offering, he instructed the brother to ask for a spark in exchange.

Adam accepted the wooden horse as if it were a tribute. He gave nothing in return.

That night, Branko crept out of the wooden horse and broke into

Credit: Karl Stojke

'Once the Gypsies were the stars in the skies over Europe, and although isolated, they lit up the night with the common light that emanated from them' (Stojka Autobiography)

the volcano where Adam had locked up the fire.

He took some flames from the bubbling crater and forged them into a rod; then, wielding the rod like a javelin, he hurled it onto the plains below.

Thus the Romanies became custodians of the fire.

They take it wherever they go. And every night when they camp, they converse with it as man with God.

And when it is time for a person to leave this life, he or she wears it as a shroud.

5. This is the story of Branko Theophilus who was a soldier of Adam-Caesar, yet was transfigured.

After crucifying two thousand people on the Tiberias-Jerusalem road, Branko and his centurions came upon the buddha, Yehoshua, who was ministering to the families of the crucified.

And Yehoshua told them: 'Death is a lie.'

And the words washed away the cataracts in Branko's head; he cast aside his armour and became Yehoshua's disciple.

As they travelled to succour the people, Branko learned how to find water on parched earth and how to blend with the landscape as if he were a brook, a boulder or a tree; he learned how to stay cool under the burning sun and how to keep his blood running in ice-fields; he learned which plants to eat, which to use for magic and with which to heal wounds, disease, fear, madness, even death.

And he acquired irreducible love which is the power to cherish a neighbour as oneself and to respond to a blow by offering the other cheek.

And the people, inspired by Yehoshua's vision of a new world with new selves, rose against Adam-Caesar.

Adam-Caesar crushed the rebellion. And he condemned Yehoshua to the crucifix.

Branko set out to save his master.

He instructed the Romanies to stop making nails and to destroy all that they had already forged.

But Adam-Caesar's men found a *rakshasa* who duly produced four.

Branko went to thieve these, but could only steal one.

Thus Yehoshua was crucified with three nails: one for each hand and the third, like the arrow that daily injures the sun's ankles, affixing both

*'Just like the other major group of outsiders in Europe, the Jews,
we were always on the run from destruction, whether it was in
the form of assimilation or violence' (Stojka 1994: 7)*

feet.

Still Branko endeavoured to save his master.

When the executioners prepared to give Yehoshua vinegar to increase his thirst, Branko, with sleight of hand, replaced the acid with a sweet narcotic.

When they pierced Yehoshua for the deathblow, Branko diverted the spear from the buddha's organs with his magic.

And, that night, after Yehoshua had been deemed dead and duly buried, Branko moved the stone from the tomb and brought his master out.

And in an oasis of paradisean trees, he nursed Yehoshua with herbs, poultices and ointments.

And, on the third day, Yehoshua was whole again.

6. O Del made India divine by visiting her in the form of an elephant and suckling her at His phallus.

There the Romanies, the loving people, took root and enjoyed the firm, round lips of a meaningful life.

Then, once more, war plagued the world.

The *sheikh* of the west coveted the lands where the sun rises and the *khan* of the east hungered for the lands where the sun sets.

And the *sheikh*'s chariots crushed Amengo's tribe; and the *khan*'s juggernaut trampled that of Singan.

The slain blotted out the four horizons. Ashes and carrion devoured aureate India.

With their last breaths, the brothers summoned robins and sent them to warn Branko.

And Branko gathered the Romanies and led them to Exile. ...

9. And the Romanies, travelling from country to country, preached to the nations. 'Love the stranger in thy midst.'

But the nations paid no heed.

And the Byzantines fought the Persians and the Turks fought the Byzantines and Europe fought the Turks and Europe fought Europe.

And after each bloodletting, a Rom or a Branko, even as he searched for a safer place for his people, preached again. 'Love the stranger in thy midst.'

This is the story of Branko Osiris who was born immaculate.

Credit: Karl Stojke

'Z: 5742 became my number. I still bear it on my arm to this day. Z for Gypsy. Two dots for full Gypsy, one dot was half-Gypsy and no dot stood for mixed race' Stojka 1994

Perturbed by such radiance, the *gadje*, who are of Adam's brood, sent the *afreet*, Set, to kill him.

And Set found the infant Branko playing in a field: tuning his lyre, taming wild beasts, enchanting birds and moving stones, trees and clouds.

As Set attacked, Niltshi, the wind who saves many Navajo braves by whispering advice in their ears, rushed to Branko's rescue and told him to scratch Set's leg with the lyre's plectrum.

Branko did so. And the soulless giant burst open like a gourd.

And two snakes wriggled out from his dusty innards and urged Branko to eat them, saying: 'Let us dwell in your stomach and make you strong.'

Branko, knowing that they would make him unclean, strangled them.

And the *gadje*'s hatred grew. And, as war followed war, they changed O Del into their own image and called him The Great White God.

And seeking a scapegoat on whom they could blame their unlovingness, they selected the loving people, the Romanies.

And they put words into The Great White God's mouth which, they claimed, had been written in sacred books.

'Dark skins carry evil spirits; that is why Romanies never wash; they fear water will whiten them by wiping away their wickedness,' they said.

'Romanies are as vermin on an animal's body; so their lives are not worthy of life,' they said.

'Hunting Romanies like foxes, raping their women, abducting their children, are not inhuman acts; they are good sport,' they said.

'Romanies contaminate white man's purity; to protect blood and honour, it is lawful to exterminate them,' they said.

And, as it is known, the more a lie is repeated, the more it is believed. Thus these calumnies passed as truth. Eventually, even the Romanies gave credence to them.

And so when Adam went to Branko Osiris and said that the Great White God wanted Inti, the Sun, Branko gave it to him as his due.

And when Adam, having melted the Sun into ingots, asked for other treasures, Branko gave him silver and butterflies from the east, turquoise and pollen from the west, pearls and spices from the south, rubies and firewood from the north.

And when Branko Osiris had nothing more to give, Adam

dismembered him and scattered his flesh to distant territories.

But, one Amengo haruspex, Isis, who had loved Branko Osiris from afar, roamed the world and collected his parts; reconstituting these, even his *kar*, she resurrected him and hid him in inaccessible caverns.

And there, until death parted them, she raised many seeds for him.

10. Hell is not a place where O Del imposes judgement, but a barbed wire enclosure which Adam builds every generation for the worship of *Porajmos* [the Devouring].

This is the story of Branko, the Bear-Tamer, who was born in Auschwitz-Birkenau, the Hell built by the Moloch, Adam-Hitler.

As it is known, when the Urme declared that Branko, the Bear-Tamer, was the promised Saviour, a way was found to smuggle him out of that place.

After many seasons in the wild, Branko came upon a crossroads where one path led to oblivion and the other to his destiny. Honouring the prophecy he carried, he chose the latter.

Thence, blind Yerko, an Ursari trickster who had survived Hell, took him under his wings.

And like many sightless who have instructed the sighted how to see, Yerko taught Branko his people's lore, even the secrets of Nature, magic, plants and animals.

Above all, he primed him with the Romany *Book of Chronicles* which he had memorized in Hell and which, like the Sikh's *Granth Sahib*, is divine.

And, like the eagle, Tani, whom O Del sent into the mind of Adam in order to chart the dimensions of perdition, Branko travelled back to Hell to reclaim the Holy Book.

This journey is known as The Return.

He searched the pools and the pits, the rotting wood and the ashes, even the shadows of ancient smoke.

And he reappeared, rambling and distracted, pierced and disfigured, with this very scroll, the Gypsy Bible.

Now that Adam's brood have unleashed poisons that mushroom for millennia, now that decay consumes wind and water, soil and fire; now that Gaia, custodian of the Earth, holds O Del by His sleeve and asks Him to impose the End of Days, Branko sires his people anew.

For O Del, has charged him to build Romanestan as the new ark. ...

11. I, Branko, Bear-Tamer, Saviour, attest:

In the dark days of the *Porajmos*, Rom, the Patriarch, and St George, our protector, saved a boy and a girl and hid them in the mountains.

After the *Porajmos*, Adam's brood became dejected; for by killing the Gypsies, they had also killed colour, myth, poetry, song, dance – everything that induced happiness.

So they went to St George and begged him to bring the Gypsies back to life.

St George fetched the boy and the girl from the mountains.

For a time, as the youngsters enlivened the world, Adam's brood congratulated themselves for having failed to destroy happiness entirely.

But the nature of Adam's brood is to kill.

Before long, they resented the Gypsy boy's manliness and envied his gifts.

Then one day, they went hunting for him.

Now, when St George had saved the boy, he had decided to make him indestructible. He had dipped him in dragon's blood which, as is known, forms an impregnable skin. But, deciding that a full sheath would impede his vision and so handicap him, he had left the boy's eyes untreated, therefore, vulnerable.

And so when Adam's brood ambushed Rom and discharged their weapons on him, the indomitable youth routed them; and even as they fled, one among them, Grylli by name, a viper who had always hated the Gypsies' sultry gaze, fired at the boy's eyes and killed him.

I, Branko, Bear-Tamer, Saviour, was that boy.

And knowing that one day O Del would abandon me, I took advice from Zoroaster, the sage.

Thus, during my unknown years, when I was as fecund as forty thousand pomegranates, I stole down to the sea and deposited my seed therein.

And, promptly after my death, on St George's advice, Lumnia – so the Gypsy girl was named – went to the ocean to bathe.

And seeing my semen shining, like eternal fire, at the bottom of the sea, she swam to it and was duly impregnated.

Now, her loins are bringing forth a whole great people. My people. My children.

These new Gypsies, finally rebelling against Adam's evil, will refuse to set foot on land again.

Out on the oceans, they will create Romanestan.

12. And it was time to separate the existent from the non-existent.
I became fire and entered the Universe.
In the starry depths, I reconstituted my ashes and impregnated the cosmic dust.
And I, Branko, Bear-Tamer, Saviour, was reborn.
I am a giant with a thousand testicles. Each one of my arms and legs are the size of ten oaks. And within my frame shelter both man and god.

13.And Adam's brood finally realized that their war against life now threatened their own lives.
And they begged the Gypsies to return to the land and save the planet... ❏

From Children of the Rainbow, *to be published by Saqi Books UK, in Spring 1999*

Roma, outside Bucharest – Credit: Mark Hakansson/Panos

Life on the edge

Europe's Gypsies are living under a renewed threat of violence and exclusion. Resistance takes many forms, the most notable of which is a literary renaissance: '*Achel o por maj zoralo e xanrrestar*,' as they say in Romani. The pen is always mightier than the sword.

Index thanks the European Roma Rights Center for their support

Gypsy Genesis

Once upon a time, God went walking in the world, over all the earth. He met people and talked with them. And one day, He called a Romany to him, and gave him a great big sack.

He said to him:

'Take this sack a long way off and throw it into the river!'

But God did not reveal to the Romany what was in the sack. And, as always, the Romany supposed there was a lot of gold in it. He carried it and carried it, and at last his curiosity overcame him. 'What really *is* inside it?' By now he had gone a good long way from the spot where God had given him the sack, and he was tired. He sat down and decided: 'Well, what's to be – so be it!'

The moment he untied the sack, all sorts of creatures started crawling out: beetles, ants, frogs, snakes, lizards. And at once, they crawled away, all over the earth.

God was angry with the Romany for not doing His will. He turned him into a stork, and said to him:

'You will spend all your life as a stork, until you have picked up all those creatures!'

And to this day, the stork is still picking them up. ❏

Romany tales from Belarus taken from the oral collection of **Waldemar Kalinin**. *Translated by Vera Rich*

GÜNTER GRASS

True Europeans

The German Nobel Prize winner explains why he started his Roma Foundation in 1997

Until this point, I have, as it were, merely supported the creation of foundations in my own disciplines – writing and drawing. From now, I intend to get more deeply involved, in a way that has often excited outrage and annoyance: to affirm an authors' right, as an ordinary citizen, to interfere in politics and act according to his conscience.

Let me announce, then, the inauguration of the Roma Foundation and its annual prize, the Otto Pankok Prize.

Why, you may ask, the Roma – more commonly know throughout history as the 'Gypsies'? Why not some other threatened group? Because, with the sole exception of the Jews, it is the Roma – including the Sinti of Germany – who have above all others suffered constant persecution and discrimination; in Germany, they were the victims of an extermination programme. And this injustice continues today.

While the whole world today has finally been made aware of the genocide of the Jews, the fact that the Roma and Sinti were victims of the same criminal and racist policies of the National Socialists is virtually unknown. Whenever the Jewish Holocaust is mentioned, we fail to add that the most conservative estimates – we shall never know the exact number – put at hundreds of thousands the 'Gypsies who were not fit to live' and perished in the extermination camps of Auschwitz-Birkenau, Sobibor, Treblinka and other nightmare places.

Worse still: some years ago, when the erection of a monument in Berlin to the victims of racism was being discussed, it was decided that it should be dedicated exclusively to Jewish victims. Somewhat shamefacedly, specious arguments were made for putting the Gypsies on a waiting list. Without denying the good will that undoubtedly inspires such initiatives, one is forced to the conclusion that we have not rid ourselves of this vile exclusion: as though the Roma and their victims are still oppressed by our verdict that they belong to an inferior race.

Our country's chilly attitude towards all strangers, bears particularly heavily on the Roma. Even though they are German citizens, the Sinti who have lived here for several generations feel themselves despised and isolated. It may be that other foreigners – whether they have been given temporary residence rights or live under the constant threat of deportation – are better organised, confident of support; if they are Jewish, for example, they can appeal to Israel. Whatever the case, the Roma exist without any protection or support; nor is there any state that will come to their aid. That being the case, how do we explain the fact that while we often mobilise on behalf of foreigners and those threatened with expulsion, we are so little inclined to help Sinti already resident in Germany and Roma who have been expelled from other countries?

True, we have inherited a certain sympathy for the 'bohemian way of life' from the Romantics: Lenau's best poems, some of Brahms's most famous *lieder* are are part of our cultural heritage. But when this people – who have no country of their own and have been in search of a resting place, however temporary, for over 600 years – want to settle down among us, the 'bohemian life' no longer seems quite so atrractive. These 'travelling people' have difficulty finding anywhere to stay. We even find other foreigners, themselves barely tolerated among us, expressing their own intolerance the moment the Gypsies appear on the horizon.

What's to be done? I've no ready solution, but among a number of solutions being attempted, there is one particularly encouraging initiative: I'm thinking of the Society for Threatened People. It has its office in Romania and has supported a variety of projects in agricultural self-sufficiency and in traditional metal-working skills. This organisation, now active in four centres, is supported by the German Lutheran Church, the Council of Europe and the Freudenberg Foundation. Because it lacks funds it is encountering serious difficulties in getting its products onto the market – fruits and vegetables, building material, basket- and metal-work. It is only by supporting such initiatives we can hope to move things forward. This is why my new foundation will give an annual or biannual prize to reward these efforts. Cultural activities will also be eligible as well as work by journalists or academics that focus on the situation of the Roma in Europe today.

Looking closer to home, if we don't want united Europe to become just a vast bureaucratic creature lumbering to extinction, we who are each caught up in the grip of our national shackles, should note that the Roma, who live throughout Europe, are Europeans in the true and full meaning of the word. Those we call the Gypsies are a long way ahead of us in at least one respect: they are the natural inhabitants of a 'Europe without frontiers'. It is vital that they are given a passport that allows them to live anywhere in Europe, from Romania to Portugal.

But we are a long way from such a vision. Speaking personally, I owe my discovery of the despised 'creative restlessness' of the Gypsies to one of my teachers. Otto Pankok, designer and wood engraver, gave me and others the chance to enter into and begin to understand the beauty of their lives that triumphed over the endless persecution. And without the least shadow of romanticism. I gained this fundamental insight at the Academy of Fine Art in Düsseldorf.

At the end of the 1940s and the early 50s, Gypsies, young and old, came and went in the workshop of Otto Pankok and in those of his students. They gave life to our wood blocks; they had the gift. We students were no way superior to them. It was in Pankok's wood engravings and charcoal sketches that they revealed themselves to us. Even in Pankok's 'Passion of Christ',we perceived the Passion of the Gypsies. Pankok lived with them; he felt a calling to them. For me he was an exemplary teacher. That's why the foundation's prize will be in his name: the Otto Pankok Prize. ❏

Günter Grass, the German novelist, was awarded the Nobel Prize for Literature following the publication of The Tin Drum. *This article first published in* Die Woche, Germany. *Translated by Judith Vidal-Hall*

RAY SMITH

Opre Roma

Do you recognize us? We're the sheep of India
Shorn for a thousand years, resigned to outrage.
We are the traders, dealers, craftsmen,
Withered in the shadow of history.

Now we have learned the paths of the forest
We have learned to shoot, we aim straight
If I am not for myself, who will be for me?
If not this way, how, and if not now, when?

Our brothers have gone to heaven
Through the chimneys of Dachau and Treblinka.
They have dug themselves a grave in the air.
Only we, a quarter, have survived.

For the hour of our submerged people
For revenge and to bear witness.
If I am not for myself, who will be for me?
If not this way, how, and if not now, when?

We are the sons of the Peshwar,
The hard headed sons of Romastan
Each of us carries the hope of a free life
That will not be shattered by the *gauja*.

Brothers, away from this world of hatred,
Let us climb together towards the future.
Where we will be men among men.
If I am not for myself, who will be for me?
If not this way, how? And if not now, when?

Ray Smith is the founder of the Traveller *newspaper and is on the executive of the UK National Gypsy Council.*

DONALD KENRICK

How many roads

The Gypsies of eastern Europe have become scapegoats for the ills of post-communist society; governments do little to combat the attacks and pogroms that have become commonplace. When they flee to the West, they are not welcome in countries where centuries-old discrimination against Europe's largest – and one of its oldest – minorities still persists

In 1994 I concluded a short article for *Index* with the words: 'Emigration may be the solution for some [Romanies in eastern Europe] but for most the hope must be that social and economic conditions can be improved in the countries where they have lived for many generations. Otherwise, neither visa controls nor frontiers will stop a new migration of the Romanies.'

Four years later, nothing has been done to ameliorate their situation and we have seen new waves of emigration. Well over 1,000 Gypsies from the Czech and Slovak Republics fled to Canada at the end of 1997 and a similar number tried to claim asylum in the United Kingdom. Margareta Reiznerova, head of the Slovak Writers Union, has sought refuge in Belgium. The steady flow of asylum seekers from Poland continues; Romanian Gypsies are reaching the West in larger numbers; and Britain now has Gypsies from as far away as Uzbekistan and Kazakhstan seeking to stay as refugees.

Racism against Gypsies shows no signs of abating and the majority of the new democratically elected governments in the East have neither the will nor the ability to change popular attitudes. Some are making desperate attempts, as they know that admission to the European Union depends partly on improving the living conditions of their Romany minorities. Western European leaders have no wish to see a mass immigration of two to three million Gypsies, ready to take any job, even if low paid, and possibly adding to the nomadic population.

A chronology of some of the events of the years 1994-97 gives some idea of the continuing pattern of incidents (see p66). 1998 is proving to be no exception:

● In the Czech Republic, in January, a Romany home in Krnow was fire-bombed and a woman of 48 seriously burnt. The next month, Helena Bihariova, a 26-year-old mother of four, was beaten and thrown into the river by skinheads and drowned.

● In May, a Romany man was beaten up by skinheads in Orlova and left unconscious in the middle of the road where he was run over and killed by a lorry. In June, a 24-year-old Romany was hospitalised after an attack by a skinhead youth in the railway station of Kolin.

● In Slovakia, on 16 May, a 16-year-old Romany boy was beaten up by an older Slovak man in Lucenec. The police refused to take up the case.

● Bulgarian skinheads attacked Gypsy children in Dupnitza, Bulgaria, in May throwing one 15-year-old boy to his death from a window.

In many towns in eastern Europe Gypsies are under a virtual curfew, fearing to go out at night in case they meet up with skinhead bands.

Anti-Gypsyism is not a new phenomenon. Soon after the first arrival of the Gypsies in Europe we find antagonistic sentiments expressed. They are invariably connected with the Romanies' colour – they are dark of skin – or their nomadism. In 1417, the monk Cornerius reported 'their most ugly faces, black like those of Tartars'. A century earlier, Simon Simeonis was writing of the Gypsies he met in Crete: 'They seldom remain in one place, never more than 30 days, but they set off, always moving around and in a hurry, as if cursed by God'.

As the nation states of Europe formed they tried to ensure ethnic conformity. Gypsies were expelled on pain of death. When this policy proved ineffective because the countries to which they were driven sent them back in turn, assimilation became the goal. The Gypsy language was banned in Spain and Hungary, their dress outlawed in Portugal; in Romania they were reduced to a form of slavery. None of this succeeded in destroying the Gypsies' identity. One reason for this was the refusal of majority society to integrate them. They were confined to ghettos outside the towns or forced into perpetual nomadism.

In the beginning of the nineteenth century we still find extreme prejudice and worse. Nineteen Slovak Gypsies were accused and tried for cannibalism in a court in Kosice in 1924 (and eventually found not guilty). Four years later, a pogrom took place against Gypsies in Pobedim, Slovakia, after some crops had been pilfered. Villagers killed four adults and two children and wounded 18 more.

The Nazi regime in Germany proceeded against the Gypsies with the same vigour as against Jews. Germany's ally Romania expelled several thousand Gypsies to the lands they had captured in the Ukraine and left them there to starve. Barely a few thousand returned. The puppet state of Croatia established a concentration camp at Jasenovac where more than 28,000 Romanies died, a larger number than the deaths in the infamous Gypsy section at Auschwitz. Some 200,000 deaths have been documented and the International Romani Union estimates that as many as half a million Gypsies may have perished during World War II.

Under communism, Gypsies were given theoretical equality: they were to be treated as any other citizen. This meant in practice that their own language and culture were suppressed and the nomads had the wheels removed from their wagons. Self-employment was banned and Gypsies forced into factories, often to non-existent jobs. Young women who wished to stay at home until marriage in accordance with Romany tradition were classed as workshy and treated as criminals.

Nor did communism do anything to counter the popular speech that ensured the continuation of anti-Gypsy feelings. In Bulgaria, conversations often included derogatory references to Gypsies: 'It sounds as if a hundred Gypsies are talking at your end,' I was told during a phone conversation with a bad connection; *tsiganka* (Gypsy woman) is the name used for a primitive stove hot to the touch and *tsiganska rabota* (Gypsy work) means 'dirty work'. Many pejorative expressions are used in everyday Hungarian, for instance, '*nem úgy verik a cigányt*' (this is not how they beat Gypsies), meaning 'that is not the way to do something'.

With the fall of communism and the resulting freedom of expression, an opportunity arose for Romanies once again to set up organisations. But freedom also meant freedom for skinheads to organise, and freedom for the media to mention that the perpetrator was a Gypsy every time a petty crime or a fight outside an inn took place. With the absence of a sizeable Jewish population, the Gypsies became the main scapegoat for real or imagined ills.

The fall of the totalitarian regimes brought with it an economic crisis throughout the region: enterprises began to shed labour or close down completely; workers living in factory-owned flats were evicted. Gypsies were the first to go as they were often the least skilled, and managers would give preference to members of their own – the majority – ethnic group. In Lom, Bulgaria, after a hunger strike by five Romany men, one set himself on fire earlier this year. This was a protest against the non-payment of unemployment welfare benefits in a town where some 90 per cent of the Gypsies are without work.

Large sectors of the majority population also lost their jobs and resentment built up against the Gypsies, some of whom by then had taken up small trading and were a visible presence in the markets, selling self-imported goods. In Poland, the sight of a Gypsy woman in a smart coat or a man in a large car could draw the hostility of the general population and insults sometimes turned to violence.

Another destabilising factor was the restitution of private property. When collective and state farms were broken up and land given back to the families of the original owners, Gypsies found they were living on land owned by a private owner who wanted to evict them or at best increase the rent. The new landowners were too poor to employ casual labour – they worked the land themselves with their families – and Gypsies in the villages were left without homes, work or money. Many took to gleaning unpicked fruit and taking wood from the forests. It is a paradox that Gypsies are blamed for stealing a few logs to warm their homes while junior government ministers have sold vast tracts of forests to foreign buyers and pocketed large commissions for doing this.

The police began to see Gypsies as a nuisance, a feeling exacerbated by the Gypsies being a separate community, hardly represented in the ranks of the police. Constables showed no interest in arresting people who attacked Gypsies, even when they had been identified. Many examples of direct police brutality have been recorded.

The mayor of Usti nad Labem in the Czech Republic, as has been widely reported, proposes to build a wall down the middle of a street to divide flats occupied by Gypsies from those where Czechs live. The Minister of the Interior has – at the time of writing – not been able to dissuade the local council from this action. Usti nad Labem, it may be recalled, is the home town of Magdalena Babicka, Miss Czech Republic of 1993. Her greatest ambition, she said, was her desire 'to cleanse Czech cities of their dark-skinned inhabitants'.

In a situation with no work, welfare payments denied, no housing, coupled with hostility leading to pogroms, the solution for the Gypsies has been to leave and apply for refugee status in western Europe. The only way to stay in the West is to apply for asylum. As non EU citizens they cannot take paid work, and the only possible alternative to this is to apply to set up a small business under the terms of the various Association Agreements. In practice, however, western consulates are not processing such applications.

Gypsy children still face discrimination everywhere. Independent reports from the Czech Republic show how Gypsy children are sent to schools for the mentally handicapped even though they are normal, except for their limited knowledge of Czech at the age of entering school. In Ostrava, the 10 special schools have 90 per cent Gypsy children while in the Smichov district of Prague the figure is 60 per cent. Once in a 'special school' transfer to the normal system is virtually impossible.

The Hungarian Gypsies alone have shown no desire to get up and leave the country. Bodies such as the civil liberties Raoul Wallenberg Society and Romany self-help organisations, such as *Autonomia Alapitvány*, write reports, lobby and investigate racist attacks and often succeed in bringing the perpetrators to book. The government has also set up a structure by which minorities are represented at local level and, as a result, Romanies, although still subject to assaults by skinheads and racist police, have shown no inclination to emigrate.

Nor can we claim that the West is free of racism against Gypsies. The rise in unemployment and the growing distance in earnings between rich and poor have led to a rise in the votes gained by fascist parties in many western countries and a rising intolerance towards immigrants and foreigners.

A recent poll in Germany found that, while 22 per cent of those interviewed would not like to live next to a Jew and 36 per cent would dislike having a Turkish neighbour, antagonism towards a Gypsy family next door rose to 68 per cent. This is almost as high as the 72 per cent antipathy recorded in Poland in a similar inquiry.

Racism in thought can turn into racism in action. In March 1995, a bomb was thrown at two children who were begging by the roadside near Pisa. In Greece this year, two Romany youths and an older man were beaten up in the police station of Patras. A Romany group investigating the case gathered statements on 30 similar abuses.

Gypsies who have bought a piece of land in England and tried to settle have faced local hostility. The village of Houghton Conquest in Bedfordshire has produced as many bigots as any Czech or Slovak town, as is shown by the hostile correspondence sent to the local council:

'You are considering granting permission to allow a permanent Gypsy site. The gate to this piece of a land is directly opposite the village play area. I would not be able to allow my two-year-old son to visit this play area for fear of what might happen to him.'

'A Gypsy caravan site would have the potential to cause extreme social nuisance and to blight the lives of those living closest to it beyond belief.'

'What resources will be made available for additional policing of the village ... The site is very close to the Royal Oak Pub and we feel this represents a potential problem in terms of public order.'

'The negative side of this proposal includes possible increase in lawlessness, litter and a devaluation in house prices.'

This venom is directed at one Romany family, the father of which is a teetotal Pentecostal lay preacher.

The incidents quoted are not isolated but typical of the everyday harassment Gypsies suffer in almost every country of Europe. The difference between East and West is that in the latter there are laws against discrimination as well as mechanisms for protest and compensation. Gypsies barred from a public house in the United Kingdom can ask the Council for Racial Equality to intervene. Offending notices saying 'No Travellers Served' will often be taken down before a case gets to court. Gypsies refused entry to a discotheque in Prague have no such redress.

What we are now seeing in eastern Europe is not so much genocide as ethnic cleansing, an attempt in many countries to persuade the Gypsies to emigrate *en masse*. This is encouraged by the statements of politicians such as Eugen Barbu and Paul Everac in Romania, while the

Polish National Front says clearly in its leaflets that Gypsies should be expelled from the country. The organisation *Vatra Romanesca* includes among its objects 'a bloody struggle against Gypsies and other minorities'. It claims that the 'holy ground of Romania has been spoiled by the feet of Asiatics, Huns, Gypsies and other vagabonds'.

But like most Jews in Nazi Germany, the Gypsies have nowhere to go. The Czech Republic has denied citizenship to many thousands of Gypsies whose parents were born in Slovakia, the Slovak government will not give them citizenship and, at the same time, western Europe has put up the barriers to new immigration. Germany is introducing new regulations similar to those imposed by the Thatcher government in the UK – and retained by New Labour – by which asylum seekers there will be forced to live on charity handouts.

Many of the reported attacks on Gypsies have been by skinheads who, in most eastern European countries, are followers of Nazi ideology as shown by the symbols on their clothes and their racist chants. The police hesitate to confront them, not least because some of their children belong to skinhead groups. There are thought to be 5,000 active skinheads in the Czech Republic alone and attacks have been reported on a Congolese doctor and a Jewish couple in Trutnow in addition to the regular onslaughts on Gypsies. To the extent that they have a political aim, it is that of the extreme right-wing parties – to frighten Romanies into flight.

However, the picture in the East is not entirely bleak. The removal of restrictions on minorities has meant that Romanies have been able to use their language in public, set up theatre groups and publish magazines; new Romany journals appear and disappear almost as regularly as private coffee shops.

The Romathan Theatre in Kosice in Slovakia gets some state support, and positive signs have also emerged there in the field of education, even though Gypsy children in schools are virtually segregated. An Art School for Gypsies has been established in Kosice while the Romani language and history are taught at the universities in Nitra and Spiska Nova Ves. At Levoca, Romany culture is being taught in the School of Education. This is a fitting recompense in a town where in 1534 three Romanies were executed, accused of the unlikely charge of setting fire to the town.

While Gypsies are barred from most discos and restaurants in Prague, the university has set up a five-year degree course in the Romani language. However, ironically, one of the few Romanies attending the course has abandoned it and is among those seeking asylum in Canada after being attacked by skinheads on her way to the university on more than one occasion.

In Romania, the national Gypsy music gathering at Costesti has been revived and is attended by thousands. The Polish *Romane Dyvesa* Festival is now in its ninth year. A small number of Romanies are members of national parliaments. We cannot compare the situation with that of the Jews in 1930s Germany where exclusion from academic, political and public life became total.

Eleven nations are on a waiting list to enter the European Community. Most of them have substantial Gypsy populations. Some individuals will certainly want to move West and this should be welcomed as they will bring new skills and energies to the host countries, just as the first Romanies brought metalworking skills from India to medieval Europe. But most Romanies would prefer to stay in the countries which have been their home for many generations. It is up to the western powers, the European Union and the Council of Europe to exert pressure on the aspirants for EU membership to introduce legal and administrative measures that will give their large Gypsy populations equal rights and opportunities in the new millennium. ❑

DK

Reparations

After the liberation of Europe in 1945, individual Jewish victims received compensation for their sufferings, and global reparations were paid to community organisations to cover those who had died with no surviving relatives.

For German Gypsies of the Rom and Sinti clans, obtaining compensation was not so easy. The German courts at first ruled that Gypsies had not been put into concentration camps for racial reasons but because they were a social problem. This was rebutted by references to Nazi laws on Gypsies which were clearly racial in their language. The courts then changed tack and, while admitting that from 1943 onwards when German and Austrian Gypsies had been sent to Auschwitz their treatment was racial, ruled that anyone sent to a camp before that year had been imprisoned for social reasons.

Gradually, the year in which racial persecution officially began was moved earlier and finally a new law on restitution enabled payment to be made to anyone in Germany who had suffered from Nazi oppression but had not been previously recompensed.

For victims from other countries it was even more difficult. East Germany did not accept responsibility for Nazi crimes although pensions were given to Sinti survivors who could prove their commitment to the working class. Some Romanies in eastern Europe who had been the victims of medical experiments also recovered compensation.

In the case of western governments, West Germany paid large sums in reparations and it was left to the individual government to allocate the money. It seems that many French nomads also received a moderate payment for each day spent in internment camps. Prisoners who were forced to work in factories have not been compensated by the firms.

In the last few years there have been new moves to compensate the remaining elderly survivors. The Swiss Banks – who still hold vast sums belonging to victims – have set up a fund to compensate survivors who were persecuted for whatever reason. One of the first recipients, Josef Lehmann, aged 61, has received a payment of Dms2,420, (cUS$1,200). Such a sum – it has to be said – would be derisory, even for Romanies in eastern Europe where the cost of living is low.

A new fund has been set up following the Nazi Gold conference in London early this year, on the initiative of Robin Cook. Governments are invited to contribute to the fund and can specify who should be the recipients of their money. Gypsies can apply to either fund through the International Romany Union office in Berlin. It can only be hoped that through these funds the shrinking number of survivors will be enabled to live their final days in dignity. ❏

DK

European Roma Populations

Albania	95,000	Slovenia	9,000
Austria	22,500	Spain	725,000
Belarus	12,500	Sweden†	17,500
Belgium	12,500	Switzerland	32,500
Bosnia-Herzegovina	45,000	Turkey	400,000
Bulgaria	750,000	Ukraine	55,000
Croatia	35,000	United Kingdom	105,000
Cyprus	750		
Czech Republic	275,000		
Denmark	1,750		
Estonia	1,250		
Finland	8,000		
France	310,000		
Germany	120,000		
Greece	180,000		
Hungary	575,000		
Ireland★	23,000		
Italy	100,000		
Latvia	2,750		
Lithuania	3,500		
Luxembourg	125		
Macedonia	240,000		
Moldavia	22,500		
Netherlands†	37,500		
Norway†	750		
Poland	55,000		
Portugal	45,000		
Romania	2,100,000		
Russia	230,000		
Serbia-Montenegro	425,000		
Slovakia	500,000		

★ Non-Romany Travellers

† Including non-Romany Travellers

Attacks and pogroms: a selective chronology 1994-97

1994 POLAND Gypsy boy beaten up and houses inhabited by Romanies attacked in Debica

1995 BULGARIA One Gypsy dies following arson attack on a block of flats in Sofia

1995 BULGARIA Angel Angelov shot by police in Nova Zagora

1995 CZECH REPUBLIC Tibor Berki killed by skinheads in Zdár Sázavou

1995 HUNGARY Gypsies attacked and injured in Kalocsa

1995 POLAND Gypsy couple murdered in Pabianice

1995 POLAND Grota Bridge settlement of Romanian Gypsies in Warsaw dispersed by police Residents deported across border to Ukraine

1995 SLOVAKIA Mario Goral burned to death by skinheads in Ziar nad Hronom

1995 TURKEY Zehala Baysal dies in police custody in Istanbul

1996 ALBANIA Fatmir Haxhiu dies of burns after a racist attack

1996 AUSTRIA Nicola Jevremovic and his wife beaten by police after a traffic incident

1996 BULGARIA Kuncho Anguelov and Kiril Perkov, deserters from the army, shot and killed by military police

1996 BULGARIA Three Romanies beaten up by skinheads in Samokov

1996 BULGARIA Petra Stoyanova shot dead by police in Rakovski

1996 CZECH REPUBLIC Romany children banned from using swimming pool in Kladno

1996 MACEDONIA Romany woman dies after beating by police in Skopje

1996 POLAND Houses occupied by Romanies attacked in Wiebodzice

1996 ROMANIA Twenty-one Romany houses burned down in Curtea de Arges

1996 ROMANIA Mircea-Muresul Mosor shot and killed by the chief of police in Valcele

1996 SERBIA Attack on Gypsies in Kraljevo

1996 SLOVAKIA An 18-year-old Romany youth was beaten to death by skinheads in Poprad

1996 SLOVAKIA Jozef Miklos dies when his house is set on fire in Zalistie

1996 TURKEY Five thousand evicted from Selamsiz quarter of Istanbul

1996 UKRAINE Mrs H raped by police in Mukacevo

1996 UKRAINE Two brothers shot by police in the Romany settlement in Velikie Beryezni

1997 HUNGARY (Jan) Fine increased on appeal for the owner of an inn in Pecs who had discriminated against Romanies

1997 ROMANIA (Jan) Mob attacks Gypsy houses in Tanganu village

1997 UKRAINE (Jan) Gypsies beaten by police in four separate incidents in Uzhorod

1997 BULGARIA (Feb) Killing of three Gypsies by police reported. Police attack the Gypsy quarter in Pazardjik

1997 CZECH REPUBLIC (Feb) Appeals court in Pilsen quashes acquittal of inn owner Ivo Blahout on a charge of discrimination

1997 HUNGARY (Feb) Gypsies beaten up in police station in Szombathely and in a police car in Mandatany in a separate incident

1997 CZECH REPUBLIC (March) Four skinheads sentenced to prison in connection with the death of Tibor Danihel

1997 POLAND (June) Romanies attacked in Wiebodzice

1997 CZECH REPUBLIC (June) Ladimir Jano beaten up by gang of 15 men in Klatovy

1997 BULGARIA (July) 41-year-old Romany man beaten up by skinheads in Sliven

1997 SLOVAKIA (August) Romany man beaten to death by skinheads in Banska Bystrica

1997 CZECH REPUBLIC (Sep) Erika Gaborava shot by a skinhead in Domaziic ❏

DK

The Romani Language

Romani is related to Punjabi and Hindi and travelled with the Gypsies from India. On the way new vocabulary was absorbed from other languages. From Persian came the popular word *baht* meaning 'luck' while Greek provided *drom*, meaning a paved road. Romani was probably one language at the time of entry to Europe but has since split into dialects, largely as a result of the influence of the majority languages of the countries where Romanies live. Linguists' estimates range between 13 and over 30 different dialects, spoken by some 80 per cent of the Romany population.

Romani is an inflected language, so the endings of words change to express concepts such as plurals and cases (as in Latin).

Me dikhava e chaves means 'I see the boy', but 'The boy sees me' is *O chavo dikhela man*.

At the Fourth World Romany Congress held near Warsaw in 1990, a decision was taken to introduce a common orthography to unify the dialects. Until then Romani had been written in different ways in various countries, usually influenced by the alphabets of the majority language. Although the Congress accepted the proposed spelling system with few abstentions, it has not yet won wide acceptance.

The first substantive written literature in Romani by Gypsies dates from the 1920s when a number of monolingual or bilingual magazines and books were produced in eastern Europe. After a hiatus during World War II and the attempted genocide of the Romanies, literary use of Romani started again. Apart from the periodical press, several novels, autobiographies and collections of short stories have been published as well as legends and poetry. Original and translated plays are performed and several translations of the New Testament have been made. The Pralipe Theatre based in Mulheim, Germany, has performed Shakespeare's *Othello* and *Romeo and Juliet* in translation. ❏

Donald Kenrick *has recently retired from a career as an organiser of adult education during which he pioneered basic education courses for Gypsies and training courses for those working with them. He was at one time honorary secretary of the British Gypsy Council and was an official interpreter at three World Romany Congresses. He has travelled widely in eastern Europe and written extensively on the history, language and social situation of the Romanies.*

Romany boys, Skopje, Macedonia – Credit: Melanie Friend

LEKSA MANUSH

Romany Ramayana

1   God is only one, oh Romanies, but He has many faces,
That's why, oh fellows, God has many names.

2   Who is Brahma, Visnu, Siva? This is the trinity, the unity of the three!
Trimurti - so their unity is called in Sanskrit.

3   God has many faces.....Who will count all of them?
God is in everything, a man sees all around.

4   The sun is up in the sky, long ago it was called Surya.
The fire is down on the earth, in Sanskrit it is called Agni.

5   The sun, the fire, the forest and every tree in the forest -
these are God's faces.
The high mountain, the Himalayas and the snows are also his faces.

6   He lives in beasts, he lives in us,
He is in you, he is in me, he is in all people.

7   He is called Siva, when he is good and gives to everybody
Kindness and happiness, when he is a good friend to us.

8   Also he is called Bhairava, when he is evil in his soul,
when he frightens everybody, when his face is terrible.

9   He is also called Nataraja, that means the Master of Dance.
There is also another name of our Master, that of Isa or Ishvara.

10   Also he is called Mahakala, but this is in Sanskrit.
      In Romany it is Baro Kalo and this is also Indian.

11   He is a man, a Husband and a Father, and he has a Wife too.
      He is a God, but also he is a Man, and he has everything a man
      has.

12   His wife also has hundred hundreds of names, but out of all them
      The nearest for us is the name Kali who comes from the
      mountains.

13   She is a daughter of the Himalayas and is called Himalaya-Suta.
      Also Parvati, that means the One of the Mountains; and she is
      awful.

14   Under the name of Bhairavi, when she walks
      With the trisula, with the Trident in her arms.

15   She is called Patra-Devi, when as a festive Patradi she comes
      To the Romanies, cheering them up with beautiful songs.

16   Kala, Krishna, Rama – these three Sanskrit names, these godlike
      names
      Are translated into Romany 'Kalo' that means Black. ...

26   God is only one, oh Romanies, but he has many faces,
      That's why, oh fellows, God has many names. ❑

From the introduction to Romani Ramayana vaj Pheniben pal e
Ramaste/The Romany Ramayana, *first published in* Roma, *Chandigarh,
India in January 1990. Introduction and trnslation by* **Leksa Manush**.

ATTILA BALOGH

Playback

> *Message*
> *Dinner is in the fridge*
> *Gran has died*
> *I have taken the dog for a walk*
> *Love Dad*

Does the quantity of information morally influence its content? Or, put another way, is the length of a message more potent than its meaning? Do messages arrange themselves by right, need, ability; or does the message giver pre-select the subject matter according to his rights, needs, abilities or sometimes even dictatorship?

The dinner really is in the refrigerator.

Gran really has died (note the Death Certificate and the tasteful engravings on the urn containing her ashes).

The dog, to our great annoyance, can indeed take itself for a walk in elegant parks amongst the trees which provide for its basic needs while we gad about after it with our dodgy pacemakers.

Papa's kiss is only a traditional hypocrisy of a superior, of the bread winner and the bringer of today's news; it is as if Papa was the State.

The puckered lips of the parental state are vegetarian. Like a plant-eating dinosaur, it prevents the milk of the female from the reaching the throats of children desirous of animal protein. It also ignores the other relatives whose tastes are different.

The state, as a collected heap of family units, has, as a rule, a single cultural and economic origin. Therefore, to stand to one side, by claiming our rights as individuals, produces those characteristics of a minority (at the social level) or of mental illness at the level of the individual.

It seems the world's newshounds have been struck dumb. Multinational companies form, overturning the economic aspect of ethnicity; English wool, Scotch whisky, musical Hungarian Gypsies, Brussels lace, Spanish flu, Russian vodka. Inter-ethnic environmental sexuality touches personal relationships: everyone can meet down at the global village disco.

Authorised by racism, the Ministry for Foreign Trade of Centraleurope Land exports its Gypsies to the slave market in Dover where they are disconnected from the respirator of their homeland. In the confusion of their coma, the Gypsies are made models of unpatriotism. Gentle English men and women, for your delight and delectation we offer you Gypsies at the most competitive prices – no need to provide a receipt. Meanwhile, at one of London's most fashionable cinemas, the already emancipated civil rights activists, clutching onions, blub their way through Tony Gatliff's latest heart-rending account of the Gypsies' problems, now trivialised for the mass market. But they only see the virtual world projected on the silver screen. Not one of them went to Dover, not even to shop.

In the aftermath of a few good conferences, the solidarity of the Play-Back button allows us to sing the songs of the slaves and of those who live on reservations, according to which there is no God, there is no homeland but there are plenty of scholars colonising the area of folklore research.

We simulate the abandonment of family ties when, standing at the back of an elegant erotic disco, we let our eyes wander after a pretty piece of skirt. The forsaking of nation can also be ensured without the severity or science of a Mengele when, thanks to cloning, a large number of Gypsies can become acquainted with Norwegians.

Does it have any cultural-anthropological value, is it a cultural-anthropological activity if, despite my Gypsiness, I choose a Magyar woman? If we do not take account of love, the answer is yes.

Leaving aside the professional advice of geneticists and anthropologists, I avoided the girls from the slums and the young scientists so keen to stuff a microphone into their mouths. My halting search for love and a home lead me to the castle of a Hungarian aristocrat. At first there was panic but my winning personality and classical good looks meant I could quickly overcome the divide between our two cultures. Thanks to my exotic physiognomy and the typically

Aryan cranial development I was offered coffee and even a bite to eat.

Greedily I took in the, for me, strange but nevertheless entertaining cultural items around me. I noticed, for instance, that to clean their bodies they used reduced-froth bioactive soap; the cleansing of their corrupt spirits, however, they leave to civil servants and tolerant judges. They don't pick their teeth in public and will only blow their nose into a monogrammed handkerchief with the head turned slightly to one side (in the way that Gypsies spit in the street). Children of different sexes and adults bathe separately in order to avoid too early a realisation of something essential. The sign of their civilisation is that they stare at a plastic box through ultra-violet eyeglasses and watch a never-ending story divided up into hundreds of episodes. Because of the structure of their early history, the problem of spiritual degeneration had been solved: the televisual smog that clings to their optic nerve obscures introspection.

There was once a king of Hungary who, as a result of diplomatic scheming, received his crown not from the Emperor of Byzantium, but from the Holy Roman Emperor. Thus Christianity came to Hungary as an alien but necessary culture and administrative system. The king instructed his successors to welcome foreigners because a state with only one language and one culture would be doomed to decline.

The poor king never knew that the Treaty of Trianon that followed the end of World War I would not only divide the settled and tolerated foreigners from their homeland, but also many Magyars as well as some Gypsies with their prosthetic identity as Hungarian speakers. Dear friends, the Magyars won every battle but failed to win a single war. Clearly, as a strategic model, this sends an important message to the Gypsy intelligentsia.

Our modern-day little kings are now obliged, before entering NATO or the European Union, to fall in love with the Gypsies for at least 15 minutes and to demonstrate their enthusiasm for democracy before the various committees considering these applications. Therefore they created the National Gypsy Minority Self-Government to give apparent legitimacy to the Gypsies' constitutional rights. Well organised apparatchiks carefully oversaw the fraud of elective Gypsy leaders, exploiting contradictions within the Gypsy intelligentsia to ensure the victory of easily programmed vassals. With foreign policy interests at stake, the Constitutional Court turned a blind eye to this electoral fraud. Everything is wonderful, everything is great, I am happy with it all said the biggest of the little kings. Now the rebellious Gypsy intellectuals are lying low and, amid the strains of authentic folk music, wait for seats in parliament or jobs in the ministry to become available.

On the other side of the global cerebrum, where tourists only tread incognito, exists an imperialism. The colonial power is the Hamburger Empire, its colony, the human spirit. Synthetic analysts fumble with the workings of the nervous system to explain the desire for and causes of rebellion and put them down as the onset of appendicitis. But the rupture can now only be cured by surgery. Beneath the stretched skin of the bubo, dormant puss conceals confrontation between many nationalities. The sick spirit must be taken to the ward specialising in ethnic operations where the infection of alien ethnicity can be professionally removed. Eventually, thanks to the autistic chants of monoglot surgeons, only a homoenous, mono-lingual, mono-cultural swelling remains.

Does the embrace or kiss of an 'alien' cause ethnic problems? Is origin or individuality more dominant when stepping over the petrified and hierarchical threshold of excitement? Love is as much a result (if result at all) of the relationship between individuals or between nations as the product of a mathematical equation containing two unknowns, between X and Y chromosomes.

A Hungarian poet with the talent of Shakespeare was once invited into the recesses of a centuries old wardrobe of the baroque style where he was hidden away from the sight of his relatives. Beneath the creases of over-starched skirts he wrote, 'The Earth hangs in the void like an unripe lemon.' Without the aid of laser slide-rule, what undigitalised bravery and passion did it take to compare the Earth to an unripe lemon and, what's more, to describe it as hanging in a void! At that time the lemon was an unknown fruit in Hungary and the poet hardly more famous. What cause did they have to hide away the poet? Why secrete him from his cloth-capped or crown-bearing relatives who devour continents as if they were chewing-gum? Both as a person and as a people, the poet became an orphan as soon as the doorbell rang.

The school-keepers of the world, the modern-day colonialists raise the alarm against love and relationships between the nationalities in order to prove the superfluity of both. However in the desert and in the and in the recesses of baroque wardrobes the vitality of the human spirit awaits the redeeming monsoon rain. ❑

Attila Balogh is a poet of Romany origin writing in Hungarian. He is the editor of Ciganyfuro *and director of the Danube to the Ganges Foundation. This paper was presented at the seminar* New directions in Romani studies *at the University of Greenwich on 11 June 1998. Translated by Martin Kovats*

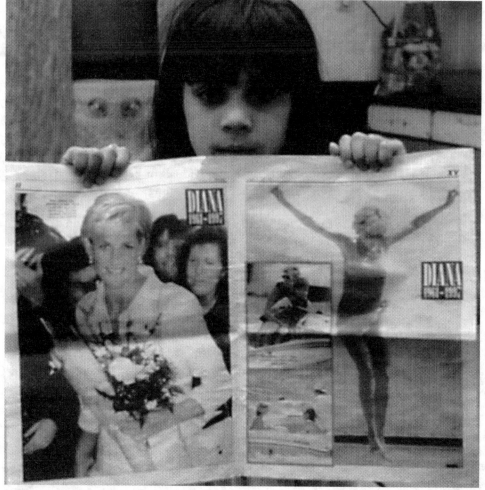

Roma, Czech republic – Credit: Christian Schwetz

CHARLES SMITH

Identity

Charles Smith is a Gypsy poet living in a mobile home in Essex, UK. He is a local Labour Party councillor and chairman of the UK Gypsy Council. Writing in the introduction to *Not all Wagons and Lanes*, the collection from which this poem is taken. Charles Smith says: 'The Gypsy community of this country does not spend all its time hunting rabbits or going to Appleby Fair; we don't sit round camp fires all day telling old folk tales while we make pegs or paper flowers. Now the truth is, just like everybody else, we are involved with today's modern world. ... I fear

What do you see
When you look at me?
Your idea of my identity
Am I the Gypsy
You've read books about?
Am I the Traveller
You heard talk about?
Will you see the folki
Not in the books?
Will you judge my cousins
Just by their looks?
Will you know the Gypsy who lives in your street?
Or the one in the butchers who serves you your meat?
What of the midwife who helped at the birth of your son
Her parents were Gypsies so she must be one
Then there's the old lady who tends all the graves
She preaches the Bible and claims Jesus saves
You will recognise her son who calls with a bell
The other one's a teacher, you won't know him so well
On a stall in the market or shop in the High Street
It might be a Gypsy who owns it who you regularly meet
I could be your postman, milkman or priest
Busman, mechanic or waiter serving you a feast.
So next time you down us, don't just look at a few
Because we are all around and we're looking at you too
And you are not so perfect to be calling us names.

that if we spend too much time living in the past we shall miss what is really happening today and if we do that, we just entrench ourselves into the stereotypes that many in the non-Gypsy society want us to be. In the West, governments continue to discriminate against their Gypsy populations with oppressive anti-nomadic anti-Gypsy laws. The British government is no exception: with the Criminal Justice Act [1994] all but outlawing the nomadic lifestyle or even the right to live in a caravan on one's own land, it continues a 500-year history of persecution in these islands.' ❑

BÉLA OSZTOJK

The Lake

Eszti Harangos had her house on a hillock at the highest point of the Gypsy *barrio*. Only the dead were higher than she and all her acquaintances lay beneath the small burial mounds in the cemetery, managing over time to move up a little from the ancient Gypsy settlement below. Down from Eszti Harangos's house lived – as she called them – the 'vagrant' Gypsies, scattered about in their miserable shacks cobbled together from mud and chip-straw, apart from the stone house of J'ska B bi, the *Vajda*, the Gypsies' leader.

Compared to those in the Gypsy *barrio* they lived like princes. Eszti Harangos often went to a lake across faraway fields, leaving many kilometres behind her. From spring to autumn there were as many leeches in this lake as weeds in the lakes of the wilderness. For the leeches that she picked the Hungarians gave her flour, dripping, potatoes and fat bacon, or money, whatever was going at the time. ...

The *Vajda* was taken to the former police barracks opposite the council hall in the village centre. Although he had turned 50 he had never been in the building as a prisoner before, fate had somehow always been kind to him. Since he had become the *Vajda*, had been 'promoted' to this high position, he wasn't summoned there because of the Gypsies; at a word from him they were ready to comply with the directives of the new order in the hope of a better life. Of course, J'ska B bi himself presented the best example of the behaviour expected. Nevertheless, in the days following the lake's acquisition as state property a year earlier, a restlessness had overwhelmed the Gypsies. A quiet rebellion was this, an impotent sharing of glances among the dispossessed, but he, J'ska B bi, soon disarmed them. They were wordless and sombre when they looked him up at his house. They arrived one after the other like seconds. ...

The policemen shuffled J'ska B bi toward the back building of the former police barracks. When they paused at the back of the yard, in front of the entrance of a small building, one of the policemen rattled the door with his fist. A few minutes later the *Vajda* found himself in a dark cell. The door was locked on him without a word; apart from the detention guards nobody so much as looked his way.

He was confined in a narrow grave-like cell. In the darkness, beneath the brand new wooden bunk, he made out an iron pot with a lid which gave off a tarry smell. J'ska B bi only realised its purpose when he lifted the lid and the stench of piss struck his nose. At some point a thick oak door had been installed at the entrance of the cell. Now it was carved with names and many lines. A sizable hole opened at eye level.

The *Vajda* tried to hold on to his patience, though it was no easy task. The sudden loss of his freedom affected him as if he had been grabbed roughly and abruptly by the throat. Anger about this undeniable and choking injustice burned inside him, yet he tried to cool himself down.

'Calm down, *Vajda*. Calm down! They mean you no harm. They are surely only interested in knowing the whole truth. Why not? There was great treasure in that lake after all, so of course it's not a matter of indifference to the state, either. And who else could give an account of the events at the Gypsy *barrio*, if not me? It's all right, there is nothing the matter. Let them come, I can only state the truth.' He limped back to the bunk.

Drawing back from his memories, J'ska B bi now stared for a few minutes at his feet resting on the brick floor in front of the bunk.

He stood up and hobbled to the door from where he saw a table with the guard behind it. Looking at him more carefully, J'ska B bi saw that the guard sitting at the table was not the same as the one who had locked the door on him. 'There's been a change of guards' he thought, and was happy to find that he knew the new guard who was from the neighbouring village; his wife was a minute-taker at the Public Guardianship Authority. They also used to come down to the lake to buy fish. Then, two years before, they had been on informal terms. The guard had the face of a young lad and a figure like a roadside mulberry tree. J'ska B bi tapped on the door. 'Karik s!'

The guard stepped up to the door. 'What do you want?' He said as if he were saying, 'Shut up!'

...

'Why are you shouting?' the guard stepped into the cell. 'From this moment on we are on formal terms.' He said. 'Are you familiar with ranks?'

'Yes' murmured the *Vajda*.

'Right, from now on you have to call me by my rank. Rule! Military rule. Do you understand?'

The *Vajda* put his hands behind his back. He felt that in his situation he could not do anything else. He stammered 'I understand, Comrade Lance Corporal.'

'Not comrade, for God's sake! I am not your comrade. It's Sir to you from now on. Lance Corporal Sir! Clear?'

...

'My dear good God!' the *Vajda* moaned out loud as the detention guard slammed the door on him. 'What have I come to? Who poisoned that goddamned lake?' The petulant words of J'ska Kingl' at the time the lake had become public property came to his mind. He said that anybody who tried to get near the lake should have their neck broken. 'Broken?' whispered J'ska B bi to himself in the detention room. 'Why? True,' he sighed and started to pace the length of the cell, limping. The day the fishpond was taken away from them, it was made completely clear to them that the territory was not theirs, and that everybody in the Gypsy *barrio* should shut up about it. The following day, the village Party Secretary said the same thing only more genteelly. Of course he admitted that they, the Gypsies, had planted it up and had brought the teeming animal life into it, that they had waded in the murky waters beyond the Szamos at dawn, and had collected the tiny wiggling fish from the nets and traps; they had cleared it out and then stocked the transformed water hole just like peasants who have ploughed their fields, then hoped to see its profit, too.

'But the world is not so simple now,' summarised the Party Secretary in brief.

The Group President paid a surprise visit to J'ska B bi; it was dawn and the dogs were barking outside. Awaking from his dreams, he opened the door and saw the people of the State Protection Authorities behind the President. They stood at the doorway as though they represented the whole world. ...

The Group President did not want to sit. ... After briefly arguing with the *Vajda*, he stated that the Gypsies, too, should consider the lake near the *barrio* to be the cooperative's property from the next day on. He also added that as the Group President at the time the decision was made he had suggested that the Gypsies who had played a lead role in stocking the lake with fish be included in the deal. However, as he explained to the *Vajda*, the leadership 'stormily' vetoed this plan of his. Nonetheless, they had voted for a one-off compensation for the participants' work up to then. 'There is no room for appeal,' he rounded off the conversation, 'this decision has to be acknowledged by everybody'.

Pale-faced, J'ska B bi listened to the President's words with a sense of devastation. When the Gypsies had settled here many generations ago the area was unclaimed. Only God, and his terrestrial authority the Church, bore it in mind for a good while. All around, as far as the eye could see every square inch had been held by the Church. When democracy appeared in the area after the War with field measuring tools in its hands to chase away lords, priests, and traders, it also took care to inventory the tiny 'island' as public property, along with its priest. For centuries the non-Gypsies, belittling the surroundings, simply called the 'island' the 'Heap', while the Gypsies themselves called it their country, their homeland, their birth and their death, and it was frequently the scene of their burials after death without the right of property.

The departing guest, in answer to the *Vajda*'s question of what the Gypsies would live from, only responded that 'in this society nobody can die of hunger any more. The people's power has taken care of everybody and will take care of them in the future, as well. There will be work for the Gypsies, too.'

The following day, J'ska B bi, without even telling his wife Kamilla, went to the Party Secretary. He came, he said, not to complain but to report to the man in power. In the old days before the outbreak of the War, long before the attack on Soviet-Russia, in the harvest season ... they had worked through many a miserable day together. ... J'ska B bi stood up at the feeder on the threshing drum, he was the captain of the thresher. Laci Ovri, the Party Secretary after the War and former assistant mechanic, was only in the third rank back then. 'Crap yourself!' the *Vajda* told him after a short argument with the same fury as the time when the thresher would not work properly for some reason. 'How in God's name do you govern here?'

The secretary stood up. He wore knee-breeches and boots. He stepped up to the *Vajda*. 'First and foremost,' he started in a quiet, educating, and explanatory manner, 'it is not I who govern. Secondly, calm yourself, because you are in an official place. Thirdly, I am only willing to talk to a calm person. Here, sit down.'

'I will not!' retorted the *Vajda*, losing his temper. 'Don't pretend that you know nothing! Do you need a fish lake? Why don't you make one for yourselves?'

'To the best of my knowledge, the group lawfully took the lake from you.'

'Who's talking about law here? What are we to do with your laws? You have taken the bread from 60 families. If that's law, then to the devil with it.'

'You had no right to utilise the lake. It was not yours,' repeated the Secretary, 'and if you want to know,' he continued, 'the Gypsy *barrio* is not yours, either. The whole area belongs to the group.'

'What?' the *Vajda* faltered, 'the Gypsy *barrio*, too?'

'That, too.' The secretary walked around the *Vajda* and when he stood in front of him again he continued, 'but don't worry, nobody will bother you. The cooperative only wants the lake. It will be developed and development is in the interest of the people, it concerns us all. I advise you to resign yourself to it. Try and look at it this way, stocking the lake with fish was as if the fields of the cooperative had been ploughed up arbitrarily from one day to the next.'

The *Vajda* was silent for a long time; biting his lips he stared straight ahead, then later he said, 'Do you have enough coffins?'

'Coffins? For what?'

'And enough hand-cuffs?'

'What do you mean by that?'

'Get some! If there aren't enough coffins and cuffs,' the *Vajda* said threateningly, 'who can say what'll happen. If the Gypsies aren't willing to quietly die of hunger, they will loot and pillage. And then pray to God! ...

At home he shuffled about restlessly, aimlessly dawdling about the yard, returning the prowling dog's nuzzles with kicks. Later, he went into the house and lay on the bed, forbidding even his wife Kamilla to talk to him till the following morning.

The guard turned the lights on. A sharp beam cut into the cell from behind the fine wire mesh in the hole above the door. A few minutes later the door opened wide with a clatter.

'Lights out!' called in the Lance Corporal sleepily. He pushed in two musty rancid smelling rugs and announced that he would turn off the light in a minute. As he locked the door J'ska B bi called after him 'Karik s'. The guard did not settle back to the table instantly. He stopped in front of the locked door of the cell and listened. The *Vajda* called out again. 'Do you hear me, oy?! Why don't you answer, the devil take the whole lot of you! At least you could hand me in my tobacco.'

In the dark, deeply inhaling the confiscated tobacco in his dreams, the evenings came to his mind when he had listened carefully to the accounts and experiences of the Gypsies who had been in prison. Gathering in front of the *Vajda*'s house had always been an unwritten law, and this had not changed after the Russians came in. Every time somebody got out of jail J'ska B bi summoned everybody. 'Listen and make use of the advice of this man if the occasion arises,' he said, and instead of chairs he ordered the gathered men and women onto the floor.

While sipping burned spirit, those who had with God's mercy avoided the strict regime of these penitentiaries until then, could gain much useful information about Hungary's prisons. 'And how should I now make use of all that good advice?' He remembered the question he posed to the Gypsies once. 'What can I do with the experiences of others' suffering?' ...

He kicked off the choking rug with its rancid stench and angrily spat into the darkness of the cell, then sat up. The detention guard shook the door. 'Why aren't you sleeping, old man?'

'Must I?'

'You must! I'll scare the living daylights out of you if you don't settle down. Why are you shouting?'

He leant back on the bunk and continued the struggle in his thoughts. ❏

From Atyin J'sk nak nincs, aki megfizessen *(There's no one who'd pay J'ska Atyin) by* **Béla Osztojk** *(Fekete Sas Kiad, Budapest 1997) Translated by Rédey-Webb*

The Roads of the Roma

EXCERPT FROM UNTITLED VERSE – *Papusza*

I love the fire as my own heart.
Winds fierce and small
rocked the Gypsy girl
and drove her far into the world.
The rains washed away her tears,
the sun – the golden Gypsy father –
warmed her tears
and wonderfully seared her heart...

Oh land, mine and afforested,
I am she, your daughter.
The woodlands and plains are singing.
The river and I combine our notes
into one Gypsy hymn.
I will go into the mountains
in a beautiful swinging skirt
made of flower petals.
I shall cry out with all my strength...

My land, you were in tears,
you were pierced with pain,
My land, you cried in your sleep
like a small Gypsy child
hidden in the moss.
Forgive me, my land,
for my poor song
for its Gypsy strains.
Place your body against mine, my land.
When all is over, you will receive me.

Papusza (Poland d 1987) is regarded by Romany writers today as the mother of Romany poetry. She survived the Nazi occupation of Poland by hiding in the forests, an experience that permeates much of her later work

ODE TO THE TWENTIETH CENTURY – *Leksa Manush*

Twentieth Century,
What did you hold in store for the sad Roma people?
Did you bring the sun into our dark lives?
Did you dry the tears from our women's eyes?
Did you lighten our songs and dances with joy?

Twentieth Century: listen to our songs.
Can you hear from the notes
how our hearts have been drowned in tears?
Look at our dances:
Our women's steps may seem as light as a bird's,
but in reality they are trying
to cast off a bitter burden

from their aching shoulders.

That burden is you,
Twentieth Century,
and the sorrow you brought
into each of our lives.

Leksa Manush (Latvia d1996) was born in Moscow and was a world-renowned Romany linguist, writer and poet. One of his major accomplishments was the translation of the Indian classic Ramayana *(See p70-71)*

THE TERROR YEARS – *Rajko Djuric*

Our house is Auschwitz,
So big and black. So black and big.
Petals of skull are hidden,
Strewn amidst the tall grass.
Prayers rise up and fall back

Beneath the ashes, beneath the dreams,
Searching for a door, a road out.

House so big. House so black.
Lightless house, hopeless house.

As I arrive at our house
My lips turn blue.
These terror years are my path;
Their names are the way-stations.

Our house is Auschwitz,
So big and black. So black and big.
This is where our tears flow,
Destroying our sight.
This is where they crushed our pleas
For no one to hear.
This is where they turned us to ashes
For the winds to scatter.

Listen, Adam! Listen, Simon!
Eve and Mary, too!
The twenty-five thousand shadows
That watch and follow me:
These terror years are our path;
Their names are the way-stations.

House so big. House so black.
House with no street, house with no address.

Rajko Djuric *was born in Malo Orasje, near Belgrade in 1947 and now lives in exile in Berlin. He is the president of the International Romani Union and general secretary of the Romani Centre on International PEN*

Poems from The Roads of the Roma: a PEN anthology of Gypsy writers. *Edited by Ian Hancock, Siobhan Dowd and Rajko Djuric (University of Hertfordshire Press, UK. Publication September 1998). The anthology covers work from the USA to Russia and has an introduction by Ian Hancock.*

ORHAN GALJUS

Balkan triptych

As in Bosnia, Kosovo's Roma are the third party caught in the crossfire of other people's wars

It was the first week of term in one of Kosovo's elementary schools and first-year pupils learning Serbo-Croat were being asked to introduce themselves.

'Your name?'

'Merita Muharemovic.'

The teacher corrected her: She had, after all, been registered as 'Muharemi'. At home that afternoon, news of Merita's resourcefulness was greeted with peals of laughter. She was the only Romany in her class and this was just one of her many attempts to construct a shared identity with her schoolmates. Muharemi was the name by which she was officially registered in her home town. Had she been living in a Turkish area her name might well have ended in 'soy': Muharemsoy.

Who would have thought, from her name, that Merita Muharemi was not Albanian? All this was 15 years ago, but little has changed since the days of Greater Albanian nationalism, when Roma were easily 'persuaded' to change their names. From the 19th century, the model of inter-ethnic relations in Kosovo encouraged the domination of one nation over the other. The position of Roma in the story has never been clarified. Roma adapted and identified with the dominant Turkish-Albanian culture. In censuses they were registered as Albanians.

After World War II, Roma were given surnames of Turkish, Serbian and Albanian origin, many of them derogatory: *Delibalta*, for example ('Crazy Axe' in Turkish); *Vragovich* ('Devil's Progeny' in Serbian); *Choulanjee* – a pejorative term for peasant Roma; or *Karach*, popular among Turkish administrators, meaning 'nigger'. But the most widespread name among gypsies was *Berisha*.

As well as changed the names of people already registered, Turkish and Albanian officials in Kosovo frequently registered new-born children under Albanian and Turkish names. It helped increase the size of their respective populations and formed part of a planned assault on Roma identity.

From the 1960s, the proclaimed 'unity' of Yugoslavia was based on a multicultural policy that relied heavily on census results. This was particularly true at local and regional levels. The census would be taken into account in the settlement of ethnic quotas in education and jobs, including key positions in the administration. If a Kosovo factory needed 10 workers, the ethnic proportions would be as follows: five Albanians, three Serbs, two Turks, one Rom (real or declared). The system created an incentive for Roma to assimilate into Albanian, Turkish or Serb communities for that proverbial crust of bread.

Many Roma did indeed hide their origins under more respected identities to increase their chances of survival, but they never fully assimilated. In 1981, 34,000 people in Kosovo declared themselves to be Roma. According to estimates made by Roma organisations the real number was four or five times higher. It would be reasonable to suppose that Roma today make up about 10 per cent of the population.

In 1990, before the partition of Yugoslavia, a diversionary tactic intervened: Yugoslav Egyptians claimed the Roma preferred an 'Egyptian' to an 'Albanian' identity. People were astonished. Where had these Kosovo 'Egyptians' sprung from? In October 1990, an inaugural meeting of the Association of the Egyptians of Kosovo took place in Pristina. The Association denied any political ambitions and claimed its only aim was watch over the national identity of its members and protect them from 'Albanisation'. It seemed that around 10,000 'Egyptians' were living in Kosovo, a number of whom declared themselves to be Roma.

Reactions among Roma varied. Writer and activist Ali Krasnici appealed to the Serbian authorities to grant Roma from Kosovo and Albania nationality status and help prevent further division in the community. But Sadriya Avduli (54) made no bones about his decision to call himself an Egyptian: 'I'll get a job and more rights. Why else would I do it?'

At the time, Muslim states welcomed the appearance of 'Egyptians' in Kosovo and Macedonia. If Yugoslavia survived the post-communist transition, they calculated, Islam would have a stronger influence among Roma. This kind of speculation was not confined to the Muslims. In consequence, the Romany population in Kosovo was, in every sense of the word, 'minimised'.

The history of the 'cold war' between the Serbs and Albanians of Kosovo following Serbia's withdrawal of the region's autonomous status in 1989, is all too familiar. As hostility between the two sides grew, many Roma were pushed into siding with Albanian interests, persecuted by Serbian police and politicians and deprived of the right to work. Roma who wouldn't get involved were put under pressure by the Albanian community, including their own colleagues and friends. Meanwhile, the Serbian authorities called upon the Roma to respect the Serbian–Yugoslav state.

Today history is repeating itself. During the war with Croatia and Bosnia, gypsies conscripted into Serbian ranks were often fighting their own people. War in Kosovo, or a larger, more serious armed conflict, would once again trap Roma between two different groups with very diferent interests from their own. During the recent conflict between Albanians and Serbian police in Drenica and other villages, innocent Roma were killed in the yards of their own houses. As in Bosnia, Kosovo Gypsies are unsupported and unarmed.

In Bosnia, Roma were returned home against their will, to find that their houses had been robbed or demolished by their own neighbours. Unlike other Muslims in Bosnia, Roma are ignored and hated and can barely communicate with their fellow citizens. At times their position seems even more vulnerable than before the war. Roma have returned to a new life corrupted by fear.

If the current situation in Kosovo disintegrates further, Macedonia could be drawn in. War would undermine the already unstable position of the Roma and a new Gypsy genocide could begin. If there is war in Kosovo, Roma will again be blamed for non-participation, just as they were in the Serbian–Croatian–Bosnian conflict. They will be stigmatised as deserters and traitors. How long will they be in any position to maintain neutrality?

Recently, a Rom from Prizen was mysteriously and brutally murdered by an Albanian friend. Reports suggest that the murdered man may have been just a little too close to the Serbian police. Roma women are afraid to leave their homes because of increasingly frequent attacks by Albanians. Beaten women have nowhere to lodge their complaints; the Serbian police are indifferent to their problems.

Refugees from Kosovo now include Gypsies but, as in Bosnia, they remain unrecognised and unaccepted by the host country. There are no Romany human rights organisations to protect them. Lately there have been calls for Roma to stay in Kosovo on the grounds that 'there is no room for more refugees in Albania and Macedonia'.

Irrespective of the fact that most voted for Milosevic and his party, Roma have no political power nor influence. They have been unable to build power structures because of the pressure they have faced from both sides. Today they are preoccupied by the future: their position in a truncated Serbian state or in an Albanian Republic of Kosovo. Their thinking on legal status and citizenship is speculative and confused. Would they, for example, lose their citizenship, like Czech Roma born in Slovakia? Their anxiety is directly linked to experience of life in Kosovo since it was 'returned' to Serbia and Roma were caught between the two parallel state structures – the official' Serbian and the clandestine Albanian – and lost out to both, particularly in education.

Nor were Kosovo Gypsies able to find the space to become politically organised. The Kosovo 'state within a state' destroyed any hope Roma might have cherished of living in a democracy under Milosevic and Rugova. Roma activists haven't even begun to talk about the protection of their people in Kosovo and a hidden exodus is already underway. Serbian nationalists call Kosovo their 'Jerusalem', the spiritual pillar of Serbian identity. But it is also 'the Mother of Albania'. The civil war over its future could reduce a nation of innocent bystanders to ashes, caught in a struggle in which they have neither role nor responsibility. ❏

Orhan Galjus is the founder of Patrin, *an international bilingual magazine edited by Roma journalists. Translated from Romany by Erika Godlova.*

EMILIAN NICHOLAE

Green summer

Summer has long gone, the autumn leaves have scattered as well, and winter's flakes are firmly established in their immaculate kingdom.

Summer, why has that season come to mind? I know why, because it was two summers which I remember as being those that left a mark on my childhood and then on my youth. I was sixteen years old, I was a child, I had an appetite for life. I had been bedridden for several years, but this was of no great importance since I had something to read and books were my escape from myself. The thought that I would soon have to go to hospital to have my plaster cast removed made my forget the torment from which I had been suffering for a number of years; another check-up among the many over the last two years, and one that unfortunately would not be the last. The check-up left me without my cast for a few days so that air could get to my limbs; that is they blessed me with two crutches and the chance to go out into the hospital's park to sit in the open.

The period of adjustment to my new legs did not last very long. I befriended them after a day of trials in which I spent more time jumping with my good leg than relying on the crutches.

I was lucky that the ward was large, with many beds which I could hold onto to stop me falling. Eventually I succeeded in walking with my crutches.

— What are you up to, aren't you going outside? It was a question which made me tremble.

— Well, er, I'm afraid doctor.

— There's no need to be afraid, after all you are in a hospital.

This was the dialogue with the doctor who kept me in plaster for another two and a half years, years in which he shamelessly squeezed dad dry of money, money for which he left me disabled. He never lost a chance to tell my father every time he met him that the Gypsies had money and gold. I dragged myself hastily into the park.

Imagine that you are confined to bed for several years, that you can only see the sky from the arms of your parents who carry you to a makeshift bed in the shade of a weeping-willow. A willow which you had planted by the well in the yard a few years before that particular moment. The picture which you have of the world, about life, is different from that you see when you stand upright.

Imagine a summer morning, when everything is green, the grass, the trees, and the flowers are in their full splendour. The chestnuts with their large dark-green leaves, with their cluster of white blossom, the lilacs, the little fir trees behind which the children hide, children who are full of life, who live their childhood to the full. Imagine a clear sky with white clouds on which the angels walk.

I know that I have known that feeling and that I have been gripped by it. It was something indefinable, there was something in me which gave power and colour to my desire to live. That desire had blossomed like the flowers, like the green which had something divine about it. I was engulfed by the green and by the sun's rays, whose rays were my rays. I felt like running, never stopping, gathering everything in my arms, I felt like shouting, 'I'm alive, I'm alive.'

I sank to the grass, I embraced it in my arms, I kissed the earth, and I thanked the Lord for that moment he offered to me. I was in love with everything I saw and I felt that I was a person again. I was lost in the joy of meeting life yet again. My soul and imagination soared, I felt that thousands of stars were around me, and I felt that heat of the sun which warmed my frail body. I needed air and freedom.

There had awoken in me that ancestral dream of being free, of being in the midst of nature, of hearing the song of the wind, the bell of time, and the voice of life. I needed the freedom which my grandparents once had. I felt the need to hear the hammer in the hands of my ancestors, in my father's hands, to see his face blackened by the soot of his labour, I felt the need to kiss the hands which had raised me. I felt love rising in me, it was boundless.

How humble I felt in the face of life. I pleaded to live in order to illuminate my soul which for years had dreamt of freedom. I felt the humility of the moment which I was living so deeply that my soul ached. And yet the life in me was more powerful than the physical suffering which had crushed me for so many years. I humbled myself in begging for life and my understanding assumed new dimensions.

I loved the humility of my people, a humility which I understood so well, a humility with which our people had survived thousands of years without anyone bowing down before us. Even though we were slaves we kept our language and our culture. A humility which meant life and liberty, a liberty which only we could understand. It is strange to love humility. I love it because I understand it. It was not the humility of a people which falls to its knees in order to seek pity, but it is the intelligence of a people that does not want to die. A people which has lived in superstition, a people which had grown and lived on the land of others, being forced to humble itself in order to be accepted. Humility was its only chance of survival.

I loved and love my people's philosophy which is so simple and yet so difficult. I love the fire which allowed us to eat, which gave us heat, which blackened us with smoke and destroyed us. I love the fire which is in our souls. The fire which has seen our love, which has seen our struggle from the first day of life, which knows our lost history. I love the life of my ancestors because they knew how to heal their wounds on their own. I loved life, the abstract in it.

I have always been enamoured of spring. Spring which brought me out of my house every day to greet it. I would wait for it only half awake, waiting to see its vapours which dried the earth, waiting to see the grass-shoots appearing, waiting to hear the chirping of the birds who were as joyful as I was. Spring was my lover, the lover who never deceived me, who always came to see me. I succumbed fully to her warmth and her caress. I waited each spring to see the storks and the snakes; I was waiting to see them so that my superstitions would evaporate. I spent hours on end dozing, dreaming of who knows what. That feeling is with me just as powerfully now.

But the summer I spent in hospital was unique because it made me feel life as something beautiful. It was one of the few times in my life when I really wanted to be alive, it was a unique experience...It was the verdant summer of my life. ❏

Emilian Nicholae is a Romanian Rom writer and human rights activist.

Romany leave

A Romany was called up into the army. He served half his term, and then asked for leave to go and see his wife. But his wife had died of consumption in his absence. He was away in the army, and no one had told him. And the dead woman had driven all her relatives out of the house; every night she came back and haunted it.

The Romany went on leave, taking his army guard-dog. He came to the house and saw that it had been padlocked and the family was not there. He took off the padlock and went into the house. He put a bottle of vodka and some food on the table, sat down, had a drink and something to eat, and wondered where the family had got to. He lay down on the bed and fell asleep, still thinking.

At 12 o'clock at night, a great wind rose. The Romany woke up. The doors opened and his wife came. She stood by the door, but would not come in to him. He called her to the table.

'Why are you standing over there? Come on, sit down and have a drink with me!'

As soon as she got near him, the dog jumped up at her and tried to bite her. They started struggling. The Romany suddenly realized that his wife was dead. She had won the fight with the dog; it lay there, lifeless. She came closer to him and said:

'Get ready, and come with me!'

The Romany drew his sabre and slashed at her. But he could not touch her; he cut only air.

She said to him:

'It's no use trying to fight me. I tell you for the third time: come with me!'

She beckoned him, and he followed.

So off they went. She led him to he graveyard. She led him up to her grave. The grave was moving; he saw it. She said:

'Get undressed, and creep down into the hole. I've been waiting for you. I'm in love with you, and you must stay with me!'

He started undressing as slowly as possible, hoping for cock-crow. He spun it out and ... then, the cocks started crowing! And she said to him:

'Lucky you, and unlucky me!', and she rolled down into the pit. The Romany was shaking with terror.

In the morning, he went to church and asked for the priest. The good father called all the people together, and they dug up the dead woman. She lay there face downwards. They performed the last rites for her, and then buried her again.

The Romany departed; his leave was over. And six months after this adventure, he too passed away! ❑

*Romany tales from Belarus taken from the oral collection of **Waldemar Kalinin**. Translated by Vera Rich*

Cabbage soup

Kalman looked around morosely, adjusted the cover on his meagre pallet and dozed off. In his dream he warmed over some sour cabbage with meat, carefully prodding the food with a wooden spoon, adding a bit of water to it and waiting patiently for it to heat up. A sudden, heavy knock on the door awoke him. He stared straight ahead in alarm and called irritably:

'Oh, stone the crows! I knew I should've eaten it cold!' ❑

From 'Humorom', Ciganyfuro, a Romany magazine published in Hungary and edited by Attila Balogh

NOW SHOON THE ROMANO GILLIE
Traditional Verse in the High and Low Speech of the Gypsies of Britain

Tim Coughlan

This volume aims to offer as complete a picture as possible of the Welsh Romani and Romani English song repertoire as it has emerged in print over the past one hundred and fifty years and in so doing to seek and identify and explain its principal characteristics and underlying mode of thought.

This book has more than antiquarian interest. It opens a way back into their heritage for people who might otherwise, in the process of education, grow to hold their own forms of speech in contempt.

This is a substantial volume of almost 450 pages. You are invited to support the publication of this book by subscribing at the reduced price of £35. A list of subscribers' names will be published in the book, and the book will be delivered post free on publication, probably in Autumn 1999.

UNIVERSITY OF WALES PRESS
FREEPOST (CF. 1529), CARDIFF, CF1 1YZ.
No need for stamp if posted within the UK
Tel 01222-231919 (24 hours)
Fax 01222-230908
e-mail orders@press.wales.ac.uk
Internet www.wales.ac.uk/press

IAN HANCOCK

Marko

My grandfather, Marko, died in 1956, when I was barely into my teens. He was just Grandad then, and I suppose I took his presence pretty well for granted. It wasn't until later that I began to realise what a source of interesting stories his varied life had been.

For a number of years I have been collecting narratives, oral and sometimes written, about Marko in his earlier years; from talking to family members, and others who knew him, I have started to put together a picture of his life. The present essay is the first of these collections of anecdotes. ...

I really remember Marko well only when he was an old man; in fact he was just 67 when he died, but I suppose to me as a boy he seemed quite old. As a young man, I'm told, he had a great deal of charm, and was something of a womaniser. He was thin, with black hair, and angular features, and because of his musical skills was very popular. He was a rat-catcher during the last years of his life, however; his death certificate listed him as a 'rodent operator', but I don't remember him ever using such a fancy title.

Most of my family, including Marko and my grandmother, lived in North Kensington and Notting Hill near what used to be known as The Potteries, in streets such as Bomore Road and Western Terrace (now called Lonsdale Road). Notting Hill was one of the 'metropolitan Gypsyries' of the Victorian era, described by Reverend John Hall and by George Smith, and was occupied during the middle of the century after a catastrophe in south London forced the resettlement of many Gypsy families from there to other parts of the city. According to an article in the *Illustrated London News* from 1879, some 2,000 Gypsies inhabited the London Gypsyries. An interesting description of the area appeared in the same magazine:

'The ugliest place we know in the neighbourhood of London, the most dismal and forlorn, is ... Shepherd's bush and Notting Hill. There it is that the gipsy encampment may be found, squatting within an hour's walk of the Royal palaces and of the luxurious town mansions of our nobility and opulent classes... It is a curious spectacle in that situation, and might suggest a few serious reflections upon social contrasts at the centre and capital of the mighty British nation, which takes upon itself the correction of every savage tribe in South and West Africa and Central Asia.'

Marko's grandfather was Imre Bencsi (or Benczi); his descendants in Hungary today, according to Uncle Albert, 'have a travelling fair of two shooters, a big wheel and shot gallery, plus a small set of gallopers. They travel the villages and have a yard at a village called Peste [Uj Rest] about 36km from Budapest. The old fellow Imree is the son of an earlier Imree whose sister married an English traveller years ago, and worked for a time on their gaff. They have, by the way, a few relations at our park on Liszbet Ilan [Lenin Boulevard]'. (Letter postmarked 8 December 1972) ...

The sister Albert mentions was Marko's grandmother who came with some of her family and with the Kocs to England in the 1870s. Another family which came in with them at that time were the Laszlos. There was a significant influx of Hungarian Gypsies into Britain during the period, following the upheavals resulting from the takeover in 1868 of that country's government by the former nobility and the clergy. A number of these married into British Romanichal fairground families. Marko's grandmother married an English traveller, Luther, and her daughters Sara and Maria were born in a wagon in Pimlico, near Vauxhall Bridge Road where my Aunty Nell and Uncle Fred lived for many years. ...

Sara, Marko's mother, was known as Granny Bench. She had a daughter and another son besides Marko, and is remembered as being a tiny woman who had a pet parrot. She was always dressed entirely in black, and kept her head covered all the time. Marko's sister Jess married a non-Gypsy, and they lived in Hammersmith, and some of the time in a caravan near Sudbury-on-Thames outside London. Marko married into an English Traveller family; my grandmother was a King, who had themselves intermarried with the Cooks who kept stalls in Portobello Road market and who also travelled in Kent and Surrey. ...

The Romanichal families who had married with the Hungarian

Simon Davies on
PRIVACY

Patricia Williams on
RACE

Gabriel Garcia Marquez on
JOURNALISM

Edward Lucie-Smith on
THE INTERNET

Ursula Owen on
HATE SPEECH

...all in INDEX

SUBSCRIBE & SAVE

 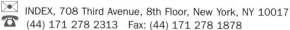

Travellers were a separate group, I remember, and it was only when we were with them that I would hear 'real' Romany being spoken by a lot of people all at once. I don't think all the British Travellers were well disposed to their own who 'married out' with the foreign Gypsies. Marko knew at least some inflected Romany, and so did Uncle Albert, some of whose letter contain Romany, Angloromany and Hungarian mixed in with the English, but he no doubt spoke Angloromany better. I remember a little song he would sing to me to make me go to sleep, which began '*mai ma maro, mai ma mas, mai ma kotor balovas*', which means 'I have no bread, I have no meat, not even a piece of bacon'. I also learnt to swear at that early age from listening to Marko. ...

Marko also knew Yiddish; for some years he was a peddler of sheet music, and would sell to the Jewish music agencies in the district around Aldgate in London's East End. He called himself Reggie Marks, and passed himself off as a Jew. 'Reg' and 'Redjo' were names he and my grandmother called my father, as well, whose usual name is John. ...

I remember very clearly their flat in Peabody Buildings, a subsidized housing estate not far from Wormwood Scrubs; there was no electricity, and the strange smell of the gas lamps is still with me. I remember that there was highly polished brass everywhere. Under his bed, also made of brass, my grandfather kept two or three battered tin trunks, filled with 'treasures' appropriated in the couse of his day's work as a rat catcher. Often he would let me choose an item from these trunks – once a boken fob-watch, once a piece of Roman tile, and to me they were treasures indeed. ...

Aunty Nell tells a funny story of his rat-catching days. When he was still new at it, he was in the basement of a bakery with an older hand who was showing him the tricks of the trade:

'Old Bill got a torch and said to my dad, 'Now when I shine this torch onto the pipes, you get the neck of the sack ready, and when I shout out, right!'. Well it all went okay until Dad saw these bloody big rats coming towards him. He dropped the sack and ran, and the rat went with him. And Dad fell on him, and killed it. And the outcome was "I've seen some funny rat-catchers in my time, but never one 'oo kills 'em wiv is 'arse!"'

Christmastime and Easter were big family events: I'd see relatives then that I never saw at other times. Marko would sing his songs, usually rude songs, and my mother, always uncomfortable at such gatherings, would edge me into a corner and engage me in conversation to divert me from listening to him. He would sing all kinds of songs, and compose them, too. He used to sing 'The Sun has Got his Hat on', 'Jealous of You' and 'Turn a Winkle Upside Down'. Hardly remembered today. One of his party-pieces was a rude version of 'Bye-bye Blackbird'. Anunty Nell talked once about his days as a minstrel:

'When I see the buskers of today, I compare them with Dad, as he used to have three pals, who played the harmonium, ukulele and concertina. Dad sang, and sold the music and words of a song sheet. He also was the bottler, and that's the one that takes the money. Sundays was their best day; they would go all round the East End. He would even get money wrapped round a note asking for a certain song to be played and sung. People in those days would throw the money from the window.

There were a lot of buskers in and out our street, such as two sisters ... they used to push the barrel-organ all the way to the West End, every day. Then there was a man and wife, with a large harp on the baby's pram. She played, and he sang.'

The accordion player was a West Indian, and the man who played the harmonium was named Peter Ball, but no one can remember anything about the man who played the ukulele. Aunty Nell referred back to that anecdote at the end of one of her tapes:

'When I told you about your grandad, used to be a minstrel, well I didn't tell you this bit, about when I said to all the girls, twelve and thirteen, "that's my dad, that nice-looking one, that handsome one; you see when he looks round! Dad! Dad!" D'you think the bugger would turn round? He ignored me, because he didn't want the girls to know he had such a grown-up daughter. That's your grandad! Now that shows you what a bugger he was, dunnit!'

One of the things he used to make was team favours for the yearly Oxford and Cambridge boatrace.

'On the boatrace days he would make a big board, and cover it in black velvet, and pin on the little dolls and favours on it. He would buy a gross of dolls, so many yards of pale blue and dark blue ribbon, and pom-poms for the head, then glue and tie the ribbons round the tummy of the dolls, then stand down Portobello Market in the morning of the boatrace selling them. Then afterwards, on the towing path at Hammersmith Bridge calling out, "Don't forget your favours! Oxford or Cambridge!" Pity all those customs has died out now.'

Somthing else he used to make, and sell very successfully around the public houses, was artificial dog excrement. He used to call this faking *jookal hinder* for the *gaujas*. He had a course sense of humour, my old grandad, and it was no doubt this that put a lot of people off him. It was a private source of amusement to him that people would actlly pay money for this. He would make several of these small piles out of flour-paste and pulped newspaper, and paint them when they'd dried. I remember seeing these objects in a row on the board over the tub: in fact I kept one myself as a souvenir for a long time. During the war, people were subject to search by the police at any time, if they were seen carrying anything suspicious. One night, coming home from his rounds of the pubs, Marko had two of these things left unsold, wrapped in a piece of newspaper, tucked under his arm. He was spotted by a policeman who, seeing the small package, demanded to know what was in it. Marko told him – plainly – and of course the officer thought he was being a smart alec, so he asked him to open it up. When he saw what they were, he bought them both. On another occasion, in a pub, some of his pals got him to leave one of these on the counter, to trick the barmaid. When she saw it she screamed, swept it up and promptly disposed of it down the toilet, where it got stuck and blocked up the plumbing. Marko was never allowed back in that particluar pub any more.

Although he had no schooling, he taught himslef to read and write, and he developed a very artistic copperplate hand. Those who remember him all remark on this. 'If any of the costers in Portobello market wanted a letter wrote', said Aunty Nell, 'they would ask my dad to write it, and would give him a guinea for his trouble'. George Marriott remembers him from his days with the travelling shows when, for a small sum, he would, with several pounds of heavy lead weights hanging from his right wrist, write out your name, beautifully and without faltering.

One show he travelled with belonged to Razzee Beach. Uncle Albert was with him in those days, and wrote of some of the times they had:

'Pat Collins, who had the Midland gaffs in England, will tell you a few more details there, as Marko used to be on the tobee with his fair at all his gaffs of top places years ago. He also got with Razzee Beach's funfair of Uxbridge Road, Southall, Middlesex, where Sally Beach, now dead, used to be gaffer, and her brother William is now the boss ... Nell and Fred did go down Kent in the 40s and you may ask them if they recall John Lees of Epping, the Palmers, Hollands, Loveridges, Biddies and Francombes who, with a few Penfolds made a proper seven days booze up every minute of the day with the board out for dancing, till nearly the whole police force of England were praying on their knees for us to leave off as they stopped all the booze coming into the village at Romford, so as we would have to go back to the *vardo*. I remember my *vardo* was taken and left in Trafalgar Square and I do not know today who drove it there. I have a suspicion it was Consuella Lee, but I do not know, and it left me speechless for £250.' (letter 25 October, 1972)

Another of my grandfather's means of livelihood was that of racing tipster. He did this much of the time, but espcially during the big race events such as the Grand National and the Epsom Derby.

'I was sent over to the shops to get a packet of BVD Cigarettes, *Sporting Life* paper, and a couple of bloaters for Dad's breakfast. Then out would come the John Bull Printing Set, sixpence in Woolworths, and the scratch-pad, then Dad would pick out the Nap choice from the *Sporting Life*, and would stamp out the selections on all these pieces of paper and go down the market, again Portobello Road, selling them for half a crown a time, which is 12 1/2 p.'

He found his most profitable times on Epsom Downs. ... Here, he called himself Marko the Tip, and teamed up with an African Bookmaker called Ras Prince Monolulu. Monolulu was quite a well known figure in his day; he came from Somalia or Ethiopia, I think, and dressed in leopard skins and coloured feathers to attract a clientele. Uncle Albert remembered this too:

'Old Marko, who was with Ras Prince Monolulu, used to go about with tips. Well, the prince did not like to play cards, but Marko always teamed up and found a mug to play the piker on the trains. I recall that. To hell with gordios, and god bless the queen.' (letter 8 January, 1973)

In fact he once had a falling out with some of the other Gypsies over this, since there was constant resentment between the Gypsy and non-Gypsy tipsters and he was accused of getting too pally with the opposition. Not infrequently Monolulu was the cause of fights, later to be broken up by the police. It was because Marko repeatedly used my father, then just a child, as a bookie's runner, that my father was taken away and put into a home. ❑

Ian Hancock, *Romany writer and activist, was born of British and Hungarian Romany parents. He is Professor of Romany studies at the University of Texas, Austin, USA and the sole Romany member of the US Holocaust Memorial Council. Edited version of an article first published in* Lacio Drom, *Rome.*

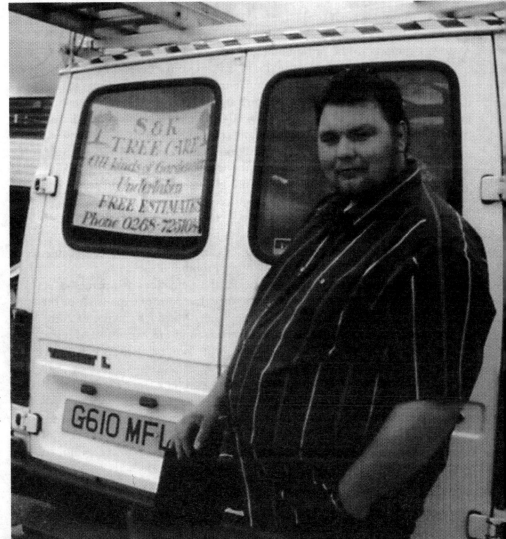

Kevin Price, UK, 1997 – Credit: David Gallant

Sticking up for democracy

Just when you thought you had finally come to grips with Librium, Prozac and Ecstasy, another miracle drug appears to transform the *zeitgeist*.

Hard on the heels of the most spectacular detumescence in history, namely the *Titanic* sliding into the depths with a pair of frost-kissed lovers clinging to the prow, comes a Niagara of Viagra to awaken the heat-seeking ghost of the male libido, an unsavoury beast at best, even on a planet slouching toward the millennium. Viagra promises to liberate man from the loss of pleasure and self-esteem caused by erectile dysfunction, to open a safe New-found-land of unstinting sexual drive. O Brave New World that has such pharmaceuticals in it.

Legalised by the Federal Drug Administration on 27 March this year, the little blue pill is being distributed at a rate of 1.7 million prescriptions a week in the USA. Though currently available ouside the USA only in Mexico, Brazil and Morocco, it will be legal in the EU and much of the rest of the world by October. Governments trying to prevent their people from gaining access to the drug will face – for want of a better word – much stiffer resistance than they encounter in stemming the consumption of any other prohibited substances.

For all around the world, men regard their erections as a natural right, more precious even than a fair wage, freedom of expression or the right to vote. The film *Titanic* earned Rupert Murdoch, owner of 20th Century Fox, a US$1.5 billion war chest to fund the expansion of his media empire; with Viagra's help, Pfizer will soon be rich enough to buy out Bill Gates.

It is far too early to say whether Viagra will be a force for good or ill, but it is quickly gaining an interesting reputation for democratic side-effects. *Newsweek* recently disclosed that former President Suharto ordered 100 of the pills a few weeks before – against all the odds and his own character – he surprised everyone by surrendering power without a fight. In Abuja, General Sani Abacha is rumoured to have suffered his terminal heart attack after taking a pill he believed to be Viagra, while staff at the Bangladesh tabloid *Dainik Manab Zamin* were attacked by a mob for publishing a story that claimed the former head of state General Ershad also needed the drug. The power to mock one's rulers is half way down the road to democracy.

The link between personal impotence and rigid dictatorship has always been clear. It was encapsulated most succinctly in the tale of the Emperor's new clothes and captured, more poignantly, in the photograph of the unknown Chinese student in Tiananmen Square standing up to the barrel of a tank. But the nuclear tests carried out by India and Pakistan in late May were similarly attributed to priapic nationalism while, in their different ways, President Clinton's legal difficulties and the English football fans' behaviour in Marseilles are both fine examples of excessive levels of testosterone. Even as Pfizer trumpets Viagra's safety record, one can only surmise what lawyers will make of future plaintiffs who have been raped or made pregnant by men prescribed the drug.

As men prepare to revive their marriages by reclaiming their erections, some female columnists suggest that Viagra may be a right-wing, chauvinist plot, the effect of which will be to overturn the gains of the past 40 years. For it is only since the 1950s that the continent of the clitoris and the female orgasm have truly emerged from the shadows of marriage, and they were quickly followed by the great strides made by women in the home and workplace. Viagra threatens to undo some of that at least by reimposing the male sexual accent on penetration and performance, rather than extensive foreplay. At a price, of course.

In June, the UN published the first country-by-country survey on AIDS, warning that the disease now rivals the 1918-19 influenza epidemic for the number infected by the virus. HIV affects one in four sexually-active adults in Zimbabwe and Bostwana, and South Africa and Namibia are set to reach the same level before long. Given the choice between a handful of condoms, useless because he cannot get a hard-on, a man is more likely to spend his disposable cash on Viagra. In South Africa, where the miracle drug was introduced in July, it could well turn out to be a Pandora's Box. ❏

Michael Griffin

A censorship chronicle incorporating information from the American Association for the Advancement of Science Human Rights Action Network (AAASHRAN), Amnesty International (AI), Article 19 (A19), the BBC Monitoring Service Summary of World Broadcasts (SWB), the Committee to Protect Journalists (CPJ), the Canadian Committee to Protect Journalists (CCPJ), the Inter-American Press Association (IAPA), the International Federation of Journalists (IFJ/FIP), the International Federation of Newspaper Publishers (FIEJ), Human Rights Watch (HRW), the Media Institute of Southern Africa (MISA), International PEN (PEN), Open Media Research Institute (OMRI), Reporters Sans Frontières (RSF), the World Association of Community Broadcasters (AMARC), the World Organisation Against Torture (OMCT) and other sources

AFGHANISTAN

On 25 May the Voice of Shariat radio reported that the Taliban had upgraded its religious police, the Department for Promoting Virtue and Preventing Vice, by making it a ministry under the orders of supreme leader Mullah Mohammad Omar. Recently the religious police made several hundred government employees redundant after they failed surprise beard checks. (Reuters)

Recent Publications: *Flagrant abuse of the right to life and dignity* (AI, April 1998, 7 pp); *Public executions and amputations*

on increase (AI, May 1998).

ALBANIA

On 10 May a bomb outside the home of *Koha Jone* journalist **Zenepe Luka** slightly injured four children. Local police chief Rebani Memsuhi said the attack was 'directed at the free press', as much as it was intended to physically eliminate Luka's family'. (RFE)

ALGERIA

On 13 May the journalist and former editor of *La Tribune*, **El Kadi Ihsane**, was arrested at Algiers international airport while boarding a plane to attend a conference in Geneva. After two days in detention without charge, he was produced before a judge on 16 May to be informed of a previous 12-month prison sentence for insulting the former director of the newspaper *L'Horizon*. His lawyer said Ihsane had been wholly unaware of his previous arrest warrant or subsequent sentence *in absentia*. He was sentenced to one year in prison on 16 May. (International Centre for Humanitarian Reporting)

ANGOLA

Human rights activist **Manuel Neto** was arrested and forcibly deported from Namibia on 19 May because the government said he was a 'threat to national security'. Neto, who has been a refugee for years, is executive director of the Angola Human Rights League, based in Windhoek. Since his deportation, his whereabouts

have been unknown. (MISA)

Simaon Roberto, a journalist for the government-owned *Journal de Angola*, was shot and killed in Luanda on 5 June. He was gunned down outside the newspaper's offices in an apparent car robbery as he returned from covering a meeting of the council of ministers at State House. (MISA)

ARGENTINA

MP **Humberto Roggero** quickly returned to Argentina when called upon by Judge Baltasar Garzón to testify during his visit to Spain on 17 April. Judge Garzón is heading investigations into the disappearance of 600 Spaniards in Argentina between 1976 and 1983. (Derechos Humanos, *El Pais*)

Retired colonel **Amadeo Martinez Inglés** became the first Spanish military officer to admit knowing about the so-called 'death flights' in a 2 May interview with Radio Mitre in Buenos Aires. The admission could have important consequences for the Garzón inquiry. (Associated Press)

On 5 May the Fahrenheit organisation and the Project for the Disappeared Group announced the release on the web of a new list with names and details of people who disappeared in Argentina between 1971 and 1983. The list contains more than 900 names, as well as information about the date and place of the disappearance. (Derechos Humanos)

AZERBAIJAN

On 8 May five reporters - **Mubariz Zeynalli** of *Panorama*, **Mustafa Gajili** of *525 Gazeta*, **Ragib Kazimi** of *Yeni Musavat*, **Salim Azizoglu** of *Mukhalifat*, and **Ziya Aliyev** of *Resonance* - were arrested outside parliament while covering a picket protesting against a draft law on presidential elections. Although the journalists were released later that day, they may be fined or detained for 15 days in the near future. (RSF)

On 16 May two Baku police officers arrested **Elmar Huseinov**, editor-in-chief of the magazine *Monitor* (*Index* 3/1998). During his period in custody, Huseinov was forced to write an explanatory document about articles published in *Monitor* in February, which the official media had labelled 'enemy propaganda'. Following his release, Huseinov was told to attend a session of a regional court on 18 May but, when he arrived, no-one was aware of the summons. (RSF)

Rauf Arifogly, editor-in-chief of the newspaper *Yeni Musavat,* was summoned to the office of Baku prosecutor Huseyn Alihanov on 25 May. During a two-hour interrogation, Arifogly was forced to explain the criticisms of the government in the May issues of *Yeni Musavat.* (RSF)

On 2 June **Azer Khasrat**, correspondent of the daily *Azadlig* and chairman of the Journalist's Labour Union, was beaten when police dispersed a picket in front of the French embassy in Baku. Despite showing police his press identification and telling them that he was not a participant in the picket, Kasrat was arrested for 'hooliganism'. (RSF)

BAHRAIN

Hafedh Al Shaikh, columnist for the Bahraini newspaper *Akhbar Al Khaleej*, was banned by the Information Ministry from publishing in local newspapers after he wrote an article critical of the 'militarisation' of the education sector. (Bahrain Human Rights Organisation).

BANGLADESH

On 19 April **Absar Uddin Chowdhury** and **Mamunur Rashid**, the publisher and joint news editor of the daily *Dainak Karnaphuli*, were arrested in Chittagong for publishing 'leaked' question papers for the Secondary School Certificate examinations. Charges were also brought against two other staff of the daily, editor **Al Mahmud** and reporter **Abul Hasnat**, for violation of the Official Secrecy Act of 1980. The accused face a four-year imprisonment or fines, or both, if found guilty. On 20 April Professor **Mofizur Rahman**, editor and publisher of the daily *Dainak Comilla Barta*, was also arrested for publishing a 'leaked' exam question paper. On 21 April the government issued a statement in which *Dainak Karnaphuli* was warned of the probable 'withdrawal of its declaration', tantamount to an outright ban. (Law and Mediation Centre, CPJ, RSF)

BELARUS

On 25 March the government forbade state employees from making available official documents or talking to the independent media. State departments were also forbidden from placing adverts, which is likely to affect the viability of a number of independent dailies. (RSF)

On 22 April the Grodno District Court refused the appeals of **Pavel Sheremet** and **Dmitry Zavadsky** (*Index*, 5/1997, 6/1997, 1/1998, 2/1998) against their convictions for illegally crossing the border with Lithuania. The decision means both journalists could be imprisoned if they violate the conditional sentences already handed down. In July and August 1997 they were stripped of their press accreditation in accordance with a law which gives Cabinet the right to 'regulate' foreign media and journalists. Sheremet is currently employed by Russian State Television (ORT) in a solely administrative capacity. (CPJ)

On 2 June the Justice Ministry removed **Hary Pahanyala**'s licence to work as a lawyer. Renowned for defending critics of the Lukashenka regime, he was said by the ministry to have forfeited his right to practise law when he quit the Minsk City Collegium of lawyers for the Russian bar association. (RFE/RL)

BOSNIA-HERZEGOVINA

On 29 May the staff of the independent bi-monthly *Dani* were verbally attacked by former military police commander Ismet Bajramovic, also known as 'Celo'. Accompanied by four bodyguards, Celo threatened the journalists with physical violence after the magazine published an article on organised crime. (RFE/RL)

BOTSWANA

On 25 May charges against the former editor of the *Okavango Observer*, **Caitlin Davies**, and reporter **Letswetswe Phaladi** were withdrawn by Attorney-General Phandu Tombola. They were charged two years ago with 'causing fear and alarm to the public' by publishing an article about a gang of youths in the town of Maun (*Index* 2/1998). (MISA)

BULGARIA

On 16 April **Yovka Atanassova**, managing director of the daily *Starozagorsky Novini*, was sentenced to a five-year jail term, suspended for three years, after her paper was found to have libelled local businessman Ivan Ivanov. Atanassova was sentenced to pay 500,000 leva (US$600) in damages and 104,000 leva (US$120) in court costs. On 2 June the district court in Pleven confirmed a three-month suspended sentence and 250,000 leva penalty against Atanassova for libel against former local prosecutor Gospodin Gospodinov, who

had appealed against the suspended sentence which the judge had imposed. Atanassova is awaiting sentence on two other cases of libel and insult, despite President Petar Stoyanov's recent request that legislators stop prosecuting journalists. (RSF, CPJ)

On 11 May **Ana Zaharova**, a journalist for *Trud* who specialises in the investigation of organised crime, was seriously hurt when acid was thrown in her face at a Sofia bus stop. The attacker escaped in a waiting car, but a suspect was detained on 19 May. Doctors are hoping to restore partial sight to the journalist's left eye which was burned by the acid. (RFE/RL)

The opposition Socialist Party daily *Duma* was not distributed on 19 May after the state printing house refused to print the edition because of long-standing debts. The paper's editorial staff said the decision served 'political purposes'. (RFE/RL)

BURMA

Daw San San, a pro-democracy activist in her late 60s, was sentenced to 25 years in prison on 21 April for giving a telephone interview to the BBC World Service. According to the government, San San was being punished for breaking the terms of an amnesty granted after a prior conviction. (*International Herald Tribune*)

CAMBODIA

Thong Uy Pang, the publisher-editor of the

popular, pro-government newspaper *Koh Santepheap*, was shot twice by an unidentified gunman at a Phnom Penh pagoda on 8 June. His bodyguards reportedly returned fire, hitting the gunman as he fled. (Associated Press)

CAMEROON

On 28 May publication editor **Aime Mathurin Moussi** of the banned private weekly *La Plume du Jour* was arrested at his home in Yaoundé by three men who identified themselves as police officers. The journalist was then taken away to an unknown destination. Moussi was summoned, along with other members of the editorial staff, to the headquarters of the security police on 7 June. The two episodes follow the banning of the weekly since 11 September when it published two articles critical of the government and the penitentiary system. (RSF)

Following the reduction of journalist **Puis Njawe**'s two-year prison sentence to one year on 14 April (*Index* 3/1998), Prime Minister Peter Musonge Mafany mentioned the possibility of an appeal to the Court of Cassation or a presidential pardon, when questioned by Reporters Sans Frontières. (HRW, RSF, AI,)

CANADA

A small weekly newspaper in southwestern Quebec is being harassed by the Office de la Protection de la Langue Française (OLF), which regulates the use of other languages in businesses and on public signs, over a picture of an employee of the agency. An OLF inspector was photographed when she visited an antique shop near the office of *Low Down to Hull and Back News* to check on its compliance with language laws. The shop is owned by *News'* editorialist, **Arthur Mantell**. The inspector, claiming that the taking of a photograph hindered her ability to do her job, has sent a legal letter demanding that all photos and negatives of her be turned over to OLF. The Montreal daily *Gazette* has pledged to cover all the *News'* legal costs should the OLF persist in its action. (CCPJ)

CHAD

The independent bi-monthly *L'Observateur*'s director of publication, **Koumbo Singa Gali,** and reporter **Polycarpe Togamissi** were placed under a committal order at N'Djamena prison on 3 June following a complaint by Wadal Abdelkader Kamougue, president of the National Assembly. They were charged with 'defamation' after reporting accusations of financial malfeasance made against Kamougue by deputy Ngarledjy Yorongar during a conference debate. (RSF)

CHINA

Hong Kong's legislature voted by 32 to nine with one abstention on 1 April to endorse the editorial independence of the government-funded Radio Televison Hong Kong (RTHK) following claims in March by politician Xu Simin

that RTHK was too critical of leader Tung Chee-hwa. (Reuters)

Professor Shen Baoxing of the Central Communist Party School told the state-owned *Economic Times* in early April: 'If we don't encourage people to think freely, and voice new opinions, our society will actually be stagnant, though it may seem tranquil.' He was the latest in a line of academics close to the party to speak openly about greater freedom.*(The Times)*

Li Peng, Chairman of the National Party Congress, called for the press to strengthen its role as a watchdog, it was reported on 18 April. 'The press should criticise the government's mistakes and shortcomings more and expose corruption,' Li said. His call came after the official *China Youth Daily* reported how officials in the Guangxi Zhuang autonomous region used public funds for extravagant wining and dining. *(South China Morning Post)*

Ng Kung-siu and **Lee Kin-yun** were found guilty of defacing the flags of China and the Hong Kong Special Adminstrative Region at a rally in 1 January which called for the end of one-party rule. They were let off under a $516 bond to keep the peace, it was reported on 19 May. (*Far East Economic Review, International Herald Tribune*)

40,000 people gathered in Hong Kong's Victoria Park on 4 June to commemorate the ninth anniversary of the Tiananmen Massacre, the first

such protest on Chinese soil. Anson Chan, a Hong Kong official, stated that 'provided they act within the law people are free to express their views on any issue. The gathering underlines the fact that there is no change to the rights and freedoms of Hong Kong people.' (*Guardian*)

The internet search engine Yahoo! opened a Hong Kong office in early June, but failed to rule out censoring politically sensitive websites from its directory. Chief executive Jerry Yang claimed that Yahoo! was 'trying to use our own judgement, stay within the boundaries of the law and try to stay as free as possible.' (*Newsbytes News Network*)

COLOMBIA

Nelson Carvajal, a journalist and school teacher who directed Radio Sur's popular *Dawn in the countryside* programme, was shot dead on 16 April by a young man who was later arrested and interrogated by the police. The murder is believed to be related to the show's allegations of corruption. (RSF).

On 18 April **José Eduardo Mendoza** was killed at home by two unidentified men and a woman who pretended to be journalists wanting to interview him. An eminent lawyer and legal professor, Mendoza had denounced the activities of death squads linked to the security forces and civil authorities. His assassination is thought to be connected to his attempts to reopen the inquiry into the 1948 murder of liberal presidential candidate Jorge Eliecar Gaetan. (OMCT)

On 19 May journalist **Bernabé Cortés** was murdered by gunmen as he was riding in a taxi near his office in Cali. A reporter with Telepacifico's nightly news programme *Noticias CVN*, Cortés frequently exposed drug trafficking and corruption. (CPJ, IFJ)

CROATIA

On 19 May the authorities closed the independent local TV station Moslavina, which broadcasts from Kutina, southeast of Zagreb. The station also lost its licence, which it had held for the past two years. The station's management regards the decision as a 'political measure', but has no right of appeal. (RSF)

CUBA

Bernardo Arevalo Padrón was assaulted in his cell by two State Security agents on 11 April after prison authorities discovered 'anti-government' messages scrawled on the walls. Bernardo Arevalo was sentenced on 28 November 1997 to six years for contempt against Fidel Castro and Carlos Lage, president of the National Assembly. Security agents have frequently threated Arevalo that he would not leave the prison alive. (RSF)

Cuba Press journalist **Orlando Bordón Galvez** was beaten on 18 April accused of giving away information related to

the human rights agency Grupo de Ayuda a los Necesidatos (GAN). GAN was recently dissolved at official request. (Cuba Free Press Organisation)

On 27 May **Ariel Tapia**, a journalist for the independent agency Cuba Press, was summoned to an interview with the head of the Monitoring and Protection Unit (SUVP), who asserted that independent journalists were financed by 'imperialist forces'. This is the first official order for a meeting with a journalist since the visit of Pope John Paul II. (RSF)

CZECH REPUBLIC

On 17 May a Romany man was killed after a skinhead attack, which left him lying in the road where he was run over by a truck. Escalating racial tensions were not helped by the decision of the Usti nad Ladem council to ghettoise the town's Roma behind four-metre-high walls. Mayor Ladislav Hruska denied the wall was racially motivated, saying it was only intended to 'separate the decent people from those who are not'. The Pilzen city administration made a similar decision to erect 'noise barriers', which effectively contain 39 Roma families in an area with 24-hour police surveillance. (RFE/RL, *International Herald Tribune, Guardian*)

DEMOCRATIC REPUBLIC OF CONGO

Peter Bohm, the East African correspondent of *Die Tageszeitung*, was arrested on

12 April and charged with espionage. Bohm is the first European journalist to be imprisoned since Laurent Kabila toppled the Mobutu regime in May 1997. Bohm, who was arrested in a war zone where rebels from the Congo, Uganda and Rwanda operate, has been held at the National Security Council Prison in Kinshasa since then. The nature of the accusations against Bohm are not known.

Suliman Ali Baldo, a senior researcher for Human Rights Watch, was allowed to leave the country on May 9 after being detained for 24 hours at Kinshasa airport. Baldo, who was on his way to New York after a three-week mission, had some of his notes confiscated by security forces. (Reuters)

President Kabila has put his inner circle of five cabinet ministers - Raphael Ghenda, Kambale Mututulo, Celestin Lwangi, Pierre Lokombe and Bai Mbayi - under house arrest. Some arrests have been allegedly linked to embezzlement charges, but the arrest of Ghenda and Lwangi may be linked to the airing of the film *Never Again*, which depicts atrocities allegedly committed during interrogation. (*The Times*, IRIN)

DJIBOUTI

On 7 May the government issued a six-month ban against the weekly opposition paper *Le Populaire,* ordering it to pay US$8,350 in damages to the finance minister and a fine of US$550. This follows the arrests of publishing manager

Omar Ahmed Vincent and editor Aboubaker Ahmed Aouled on 5 May. On 26 April the paper had printed a story accusing the finance minister of embezzlement. The state prosecutor is investigating allegations of 'incitement to racial hatred' against the newspaper. (RSF)

EGYPT

The Higher Press Council purged two heads of state-owned newspapers on 16 April, replacing *Rose al-Yusuf* editor Mahmud al-Tuhami with former presidential press spokesman Muhammad Abd al-Mun'im and *Akher Sa'a* editor Galal Isa with former crime columnist Mahmud Salah. Al-Tuhami was pushed into retirement for supporting his ousted deputy, Adel Hamouda, dismissed by the HPC in March (*Index* 3/98). Isa was transferred to head an obscure publishing board. Underlining the loyalty of the new appointees, Salah's first editorial detailed his thrill at flying with Mubarak in the presidential plane. (*Middle East International, Cairo Times*)

The American University in Cairo (AUC) removed from its library on 14 May the book *Muhammad*, by Maxime Rodinson, after a newspaper columnist said the book 'denigrated the Islamic faith'. Salah Montasser attacked the book, a mildly revisionist, psychological approach to the Prophet first published in the 1970s, in his 13 May column in *al-Ahram*. AUC went beyond the Higher Education Ministry's request to remove the book from a teaching

course, by also taking it off shelves and out of the library database. (*Cairo Times*)

On 20 May the Abdeen Court of Appeals for Misdemeanours sentenced journalist Amr Abdel Hadi Nasif to three months' imprisonment on charges of libel and slander for a series of articles he wrote in *Al-Ahrar* newspaper. This ruling is the fourth such against journalists within a period of three months. Magdi Hussein and Ahmed Hilal of the *Al-Sha'ab*, and Gamal Fahmy Hassan of *Al Arabi* are serving sentences in Mazra'it Tora Prison, where Nasif joins them (*Index* 3/1998). (EOHR)

On 30 May the *Cairo Times* was again banned from printing in Egypt in the latest government attempt to harass the bi-weekly. The General Authority for Free Zones and Investment (GAFI) served a notice on the newspaper's printer declaring it a 'political' publication and thus in violation of new publishing restrictions. Since 1994, about 60 publications have registered overseas and printed in the Nasser City free zone in order to escape severe censorship laws. But on 31 March, the GAFI told the two printing houses in the zone that they could no longer print publications of any sort (*Index* 3/1998). (*Cairo Times*, CPJ, Egyptian Organization for Human Rights)

Abd al-Munim Gamal al-Din, a freelance journalist, went on hunger strike to protest against the illegality of his detention on 9 June. Abdl

al-Munim is reportedly receiving no medical treatment in what is regarded as one of Egypt's most notorious prisons. (AI)

EQUATORIAL GUINEA

Eight Spanish correspondants, covering the trial of 113 opposition activists for *El País, La Vanguardia, El Heraldo de Aragon,* the news agency *EFE* and the TVE television channel, were expelled on 31 May. The Deputy Prime Minister in charge of Foreign Affairs Miguel Oyono, who called their coverage of the trial 'tendentious', said the authorities 'invited' the journalists to leave because trial proceedings had come to an end. The accused were sentenced two days after the expulsion. (RSF)

ERITREA

Ruth Simon of Agence France Presse (AFP), an old friend of President Afeworki, was imprisoned on his personal order on 25 April and charged with spreading 'false information'. Simon had published reports alleging that the president had confirmed the presence of Eritrean troops fighting alongside Sudanese rebels. AFP later published a denial by the central committee of the ruling People's Front for Democracy and Justice, which described the report as a 'gross distortion' of the president's statement. (RSF)

ETHIOPIA

Tsegaye Ayalew, editor of the weekly *Genenaw;*

Alemayehu Kifle, editor of the weekly *Zegabi*; **Alemayehu Shiferaw**, deputy editor of *Tarik;* and **Dawit Taye**, journalist at the weekly *Aemero*, were all reported arrested on 19 May, temporarily bringing the number of independent media workers in prison to 21. Kifle was released shortly afterwards, as were two other journalists, **Tamrat Gemeda** and **Mukenil Shebo**. It was later reported that **Abebe Abashu**, **Yadesa Bedassa**, **Alemayehu Dirro**, **Ademe Gebre-Senet**, **Sori Kitila**, **Dawit Mekonnen**, **Isayas Negatu**, **Mohamed Sheka**, **Alemayehu Umatta**, **Muktar Usman** and **Hundesa Wakwaya** had all been released following a short period of detention (*Index 3/1998*). Over 20 private journalists have also gone into voluntary exile in recent months. (AI, RSF, *Ethiop*)

Tesfaye Tadesse, owner and editor of the defunct magazine *Mestawet* and newspaper *Lubar*, was hacked to death in front of his home on 7 June by two unidentified individuals who escaped the scene of the crime. Tesfaye, a lawyer and member of the Ethiopian Human Rights Council, was previously jailed by President Zenawi's Ethiopian Peoples Revolutionary Democratic Front in 1993. (CPJ)

EUROPEAN UNION

Parliament approved a directive on 13 May which will lead to an almost blanket ban on tobacco advertising throughout the EU by 2006. Sir Frank Rogers, chairman of the European Publishers Council, attacked the ban saying that the loss of revenue for the press will result in an erosion of freedom of expression. (*Daily Telegraph*)

In late May, after seven years of negotiation, EU ministers agreed that a driving ban in one member state will apply throughout the Union. A single list of disqualified drivers will be maintained by the EU, although traffic laws will still vary. (*Guardian*)

FIJI

On 5 June the Senate accepted a privileges committee recommendation to warn the *Fiji Times*, the island's biggest newspaper, over a report which it said had breached journalistic parlimentary privilege (*Index 6/1997*). No formal charges were laid against the newspaper, but the upper house made it clear that any recurrence would be met with 'severe repercussions. *Fiji Times* has made it equally clear that it will not back down. On 2 June *The Times* printed an identical report on a 12-minute meeting of the Senate, again querying its value to taxpayers. The issue of press privilege had already become a potential controversy. In the 14 May edition of the *Daily Post*, assistant Information Minister Ratu Josefa Dimuri hinted that journalists would soon be subject to a test before gaining accreditation to parliament. (PINA)

FRANCE

Albert du Roy, news editor-in-chief at the state-funded FR2 TV station resigned on 9 June, citing demands for higher ratings which conflicted with his own intention to boost the seriousness of content. Resistance to his plans came both from state and staff. In his resignation letter, du Roy referred to the 'arrogant contempt' of main news reader Daniel Bilalian. (*Guardian, Independent*)

GAMBIA

On 26 April officials from the police, immigration and the National Intelligence Agency raided the editorial offices of the independent *Daily Observer*, arresting seven members of the technical staff, two of whom were Senegalese. They were detained for four days and released without charge. The officers apparently came in search of editorial staff, but they had already left the offices. The action was reportedly prompted by the paper's coverage of the trial of **Baboucar Gaye**, owner of Citizen FM radio and the *New Citizen* newspaper, who is being tried for operating a radio station without a licence (*Index 2/1998*). (AI, A19, PEN)

GERMANY

In early May the ultra nationalist Deutsche Volksunion (DVU) won 13 per cent of the vote in elections to the Saxony-Anhalt state parliament. The party's leader is businessman Gerhard Frey, who is believed to possess a fortune of US$250 million. Frey's interests include a publishing empire specialising in nostalgia for the Third

Reich. The DVU did not hold election rallies. Frey's campaign expenditure of US$1.6 million was instead used for 20,000 posters and 1.2 million personally addressed letters. Since the DVU broke through the representation barrier of 5 per cent, Frey's costs will be rebated by taxpayers. (*Guardian, European*)

On 28 May a Munich court gave Felix Somm, formerly the local head of the CompuServe internet provider, a two-year suspended sentence for participation in the dissemination of child and animal pornography. Defence lawyers questioned the right of the Bavarian state to regulate a supranational means of communication. Despite a sudden call from the prosecution for acquittal, Judge Wilhelm Hubbert ruled that Somm had merely 'abused the medium'. Since Somm was charged in 1995, specific legislation relating to the internet has been passed, outlawing child pornography, Nazi propaganda and Holocaust denial. Internet providers, however, are only liable if they are 'aware of the content'. (*European, Financial Times, Guardian, Independent*)

Welt am Sonntag published on 31 May classified German government papers relating to reunification. Initially intended to be kept secret until 2019, the documents revealed then British Prime Minister Margaret Thatcher's opposition to an immediate reintegration of East Germany. (*Sunday Times*)

GHANA

Immigration officers on 27 May picked up two Nigerian journalists and threatened them with deportation. **Bunmi Aborisade** and **Lewis Asubiojo** work from Ghana, where they are also seeking asylum. They were released after being warned 'to stop their high profile activism in the affairs of Nigeria while in Ghana'. (Free Expression Ghana, CPJ)

On 6 May, police arrested two photographers suspected of being behind an internet sex site in which pictures of nude girls had been used. Police said they had arrested **Charles Agbavitor** and **Stephen Takyi Nkhruma**, after a tip-off from the models. A third photographer, **Anthony Quansah**, who is now on the run, has been declared a 'wanted person'. (*Ghanaian Independent*)

GREECE

In the latest round of a dispute over an allegedly insulting definition contained in a recently published dictionary, court officials in Thessalonika on 26 May slapped a temporary injunction on sales of the book. A local politician complained at the dictionary's definition of 'Bulgarians' as a 'pejorative', slang term for supporters or players of sports teams from the city, which is close to the Bulgarian border. Fans of Athenian soccer and basketball teams often taunt their northern counterparts with the term. After provoking outrage in the north and the public ire of ministers, the dictionary's author, **George Babiniotis**, asked 'Are we supposed to leave out all the words we don't like?' (Greek Helsinki Monitor)

Eva Androutsopoulos was due to stand trial in the northeastern town of Komotini, for violating article 4 of the Obligatory Law, passed during the Metaxas regime. Charged with proselytism, which allegedly occurred when she was teaching in a German tutorial school in 1995, she is accused of 'attempting in an indirect way...to introduce pupils to the religious conscience of believers in different dogmas'. This is the first trial on proselytism since 1993. (Greek Helsinki Monitor)

GUATEMALA

On 25 April **Archbishop Juan Gerardi** was beaten to death two days after he presented a report on human rights violations during the 36-year civil war. The report identifies the army as responsible for 90 per cent of the 55,000 human rights violations counted. It also includes testimonies of victims and witnesses to the human rights violations collected over a three-year period. (AI, *International Herald Tribune*, Grupo de Apoyo Mutuo, Equipo Nizkor).

Two grenades exploded in front of the home of journalist **Amilcar Nuila** on 30 April causing significant damage. Nuila is the director of the local radio news programme *Mail of the North*, which covered the trial of an army patroller accused of having carried out the massacre of Xaman in 1995 when 11 people were killed. Nuila works for the daily *Prensa Libre* and the news programme *TV Notisiete*. (Action Alert)

INDIA

On 15 May **Dhiren Chakravarty** and **Atanu Bhuyan**, editor and executive editor respectively of the Guwahati-based daily *Ajir Batori*, were arrested by Assam police and charged with defaming the state parliament and its members in a critical article published on 21 March. (RSF)

Sushma Swaraj, Minister for Communications, Information and Broadcasting, announced on 24 May that the government would produce its own programmes to be broadcast on its international channel to counter what it perceives as a 'negative image' projected by foreign networks such as CNN and the BBC. (Reuters)

Recent Publication: *A Mockery of Justice – The case concerning the 'disappearance' of human rights defender Jaswant Singh Khalra severely undermined* (AI, April 1998, pp 6); *Manipur: The silencing of youth* (AI, May 1998, pp 10).

INDONESIA

Paul Watson, foreign correspondent and photographer with the *Toronto Star*, was arrested by local police in Medan on 6 May. He had been taking pictures of a

'store being looted during violent protests against rising prices'. He was subject to verbal interogation during his nine hour detention. (RSF)

At least nine journalists were attacked by the police or army while covering the anti-Suharto riots, according to a report on 18 May. **Sayuti** of Media Indonesia was hit by two bullets at the 14 May riot in Jakarta. **Tutang Muchtar**, a photographer with the weekly *Sinar*, was beaten by eight policemen who also seized his camera. **Yuyung Abdi** of *Jawa Pos* was kicked by soldiers. **A.R. Rochime**, of *Aksi* was threatened at gunpoint and beaten with truncheons. **Munawar Mandailing**, of news agency *Antara*, was arrested and beaten while he was trying to take a picture of a burning motorbike. **Ika Rais** of *Pikiran Rakyat*, **Riyanto Oemar** of *Republika*, **Hindaryoen** of *Kompas*, and **Edi Romadhon** of *Kedaulatan Rakyat* were also beaten by Jakarta police. (RSF)

Ging Ginanyar, a correspondent for the Australian radio station SBS, was sentenced on 20 May to two months and 10 days in jail for interviewing an actress known for her sympathies with the opposition. Ginanjar was released immediately since his sentence corresponded to the time that he had already spent in custody. (RSF)

On 28 May the government released two more political prisoners but journalist **Andi Syahputra** and political activist **Nuku Soleiman** refused to sign their release

papers, saying that they rejected what the government had called an 'amnesty'. (RSF)

The extensive media coverage of the riots on 14 May was scaled down after government pressure. The five networks – RCTI, SCTV, TPI, Indosiar and AN-teve – covered the student protests, riots and the student killings without being subject to censorship. An abrupt change occurred following an order from the then minister of information, Alwi Dahlan, who instructed networks to send their videotapes to the state-owned TVRI for approval. This government-controlled pool then compiled a 30-minute news programme subsequently relayed by all TV stations. Restrictions were lifted, however, with the downfall of the Suharto regime. (*Nation, Jakarta Post*)

The new Information Minister Muhammad Yanus has launched what could presage the wholesale dismantling of Suharto-era press restrictions. On 5 June, he repealed the 1975 regulation which made the Indonesian Journalists Association (PWI) the sole legal union for the profession. The move effectively recognises the Alliance of Indonesia Journalists (AJI), set up in 1994 by journalists unhappy with the way that the PWI responded to the closure of three magazines by the government. One of them, the weekly *Tempo*, will benefit from the repeal of the law which gave government the right to revoke the licences of media which disseminated dissident views. Nor will newspapers need approval before appointing or changing their editors. Private radio stations will also be allowed to produce more news programmes, as the number of state-run bulletins they legally have to relay has been reduced from 14 per day to four. (*Jakarta Post*, Reuters)

IRAN

On 11 May the head of the official news agency IRNA, **Fereydoun Verdinejad**, was acquitted by the Press Court of charges that he had published a caricature of the parliamentary deputy who brought the charges against him. (Reuters)

ISRAEL

Journalist **Ronit Weiss-Berkowitz** received death threats from Jewish extremists in April for her part in a TV series marking the 50th anniversary of the declaration of the state of Israel. The documentary challenges the traditional Israeli view of history, including the commonly held view that Palestine was virtually uninhabited when Israel was created. (Freedom House)

Jewish settler **Itimar Ben Gvir** was remanded in custody on 10 May after his fingerprints were found on a photo-montage depicting assassinated former prime minister Yitzhak Rabin in the nude. A spokesperson for the outlawed right-wing group *Kach* said the pasting of the eight photo-montages outside a playground owned by the Dor Shalom peace movement was 'an issue of artistic

expression'. (Reuters)

Gaza-based journalist **Taher Shriteh** declined a 24 May offer from Shin Bet lawyers to give him limited freedom of movement in exchange for dropping his High Court petition against the security agency which has denied him permission to travel to Jerusalem since March 1995. Shin Bet said it might allow him to reach the outside via Gaza's border crossing with Egypt, contravening the Oslo Accords' guarantee of freedom of movement within the Palestinian Authority's fragmented territory. Shriteh, who works for the *New York Times*, CBS, Reuters and the BBC, won the US National Press Club's Freedom of the Press Award in 1993. (CPJ)

On 27 May the Israel Broadcasting Authority (IBA) demoted two editors and reprimanded a director and news director for a report it said was doctored to show Prime Minister Benjamin Netanyahu waving to a crowd that was chanting 'Death to Arabs'. IBA officials said that while the crowd did chant ' Death to Arabs' during a victory rally of national soccer league champion Betar Jerusalem, the soundtrack was edited to make it appear as if Netanyahu could actually hear the fans beneath the Jerusalem balcony where he was waving. A statement from the newsroom retorted: 'The director general shot us with the Prime Minister's gun and they now have the entire news staff in their sight. It has been proved outright that there was "no doctoring" and no

"falsification"'. (*The Times,* Reuters)

In the morning of 2 April, **Amel Chihade**, a journalist with the Arabic daily newspaper *al-Ittihad*, was threatened at the newspaper's offices by a man who then threw a corrosive liquid at Chihade's hands and an ashtray at her head. Chihade was hospitalised with minor skin lesions. The suspected assailant is a man known to be close to Islamist circles in Israel. (RSF)

Recent publications: *Out in the Cold—The Palestinian Refugees* (Council for the Advancement of Arab-British Understanding, April 1998, 5pp); *Routine Torture— Interrogation Methods of the General Security Service* (B'Tselem, May 1998)

JAPAN

Yokohama District Court on 23 April ruled that two changes to a textbook demanded by the Education Ministry were illegal and ordered the government to pay ¥200,000 (US$1,380) to the author **Nobuyuoshi Takashima**. One passage quoted Fukuzawa Yukichi's philosophical treatises *Departure from Asia* which described other Asian nations as 'savage'. The other statement was Takashima's opinion that Japan should have consulted other Asian countries before sending minesweepers to the Persian Gulf in 1991. (*Japan Times*)

During Emperor Akihito's visit to the UK in May, the Imperial Household Agency made it known to Japanese media that planned demonstrations by former British prisoners of war should not be 'overstated'. Court reporter for the *Hokkaido Shimbun* **Ryo Aiuchi** claimed: 'We exercise self-censorship. It is often made clear to us by the Agency that we should not report certain stories. We ignore such advice at the risk of upsetting our main source of stories.' (*Guardian*)

The release on 23 May of a film about General Hideki Tojo, *Pride: The Fateful Moment* prompted criticism from regional neighbours. North Korean paper *Rodong Simmun* called the film 'shameless' for 'seeking to eradicate the guilty conscience of the past and implant pride in the past in the minds of the Japanese'. China's Xinhua agency quoted a government source saying 'we felt shocked that some people in Japan produced such a movie to whitewash aggression and sing praises of Hideki Tojo'. (*Guardian*)

JORDAN

Police threw a cordon around the offices of the daily *al-Arab al-Youm* on 8 April to ensure that it did not report the murders in Amman that day of lawyer Hanni Naddeh, his son Suhail Naddeh, and Awni Saad, a prominent psychiatrist. The paper's distribution was delayed until police had reviewed its contents. Distribution was similarly delayed on 16 and 17 April. The blackout on coverage of the triple murder closely follows a late-March order not to report the trial of **Leith**

Shubeilat, a prominent opposition politician, for inciting an illegal demonstration. (CPJ)

Youssef Gheishan, a satirical writer for the weeklies *Abed Rabboh, al-Bilad* and the daily *al-Arab al-Yawm*, was released from six days' detention on 18 April. Gheishan had been arrested at his home on 11 April by 15 security agents who confiscated his files and archives and every document in his handwriting. Gheishan was told that he had been arrested on charges of *lèse majesté* and distributing seditious leaflets in the town of Madaba. Gheishan is a convert to Christianity and after his release said: 'I was surprised by the charge of heading an Islamic opposition group.' (*Jordan Times*)

On 12 May the government ordered an indefinite ban on the distribution of the London-based daily *Al-Quds al Arabi* for violating the 'most basic rules of professionalism and objectivity'. Individual issues of the newspaper had been seized on several occasions in October 1997 (*Index* 1/1998). The newspaper's Amman correspondent, **Bassam Badareen**, was formally charged with 'distorting Jordan's image abroad', harming state relations with a friendly country and offending the state. (CPJ)

On 2 June the Amman Court of First Instance sentenced **Nidal Mansour**, editor in chief of weekly *Al-Hadath,* to six months' imprisonment, pending appeal, for 'harming

relations with a friendly state'. In a 1994 article in the weekly *Al-Bilad*, Mansour had reported on allegations relating to the involvement of Lebanese parliamentarians and the son of President Elias Hrawi in narcotics trafficking. The ruling follows a successful conviction for criminal defamation against **Raja Talab** and **Riad Hroub** of *Shihan*, columnist **Riham Farra** and former editor **Abdel Hadi Raja Majalli**.

KENYA

In April the High Court in Nairobi prohibited **Njehu Gatabaki**, owner of *Finance*, from publishing, or causing to be published, an article in the magazine's 5 April issue which, in the judge's view, committed 'injurious falsehoods' against prominent businessman Samuel Kamau Macharia (*Index* 3/1998). At the same time, owners and editors of the Nairobi weekly *Dispatch* have been restrained from publishing defamatory words against two government ministers, Musalia Mudavadi and Chrisanthus Okemo. Both ministers alleged that they were portrayed as criminals by the journal and demanded damages and costs. (NDIMA)

In mid-May **Njuguna Mutahi**, publications officer of the Kenya Human Rights Commission, and **Wahome Karengo**, a journalist with the opposition newspaper, the *Star*, were arrested after being accused of theft. Thing'o Kagicha, the executive director of a pro-government NGO, NGO Watch, accused Mutahi of stealing an advance copy of a confidential report and some personal property. Mutahi said that he had been given the report by Karengo. (AI)

KYRGYZSTAN

On 1 May **Yodgar Parpiev** of the regional human rights organisation *Spravedlivost* (Justice) was arrested in the village of Masy, Jalal-Abad by officers of the Nookenskov Regional Department of Internal Affairs (RDIA). During his detention he was reportedly abused by the employees and manager U. Aytbaev of the RDIA. Parpiev is currently facing an administrative charge of 'internally disobeying the legal orders or demands of an officer of the authorities of internal affairs'. (Bureau on Human Rights and Rule of Law)

Following the publication of an article entitled '*Jihad Victims and Hostages*' in *Vecherny Bishkek* on 1 May, the Spiritual Board of Muslims in Kyrgyzstan made an appeal on 12 May in which it accused Russians and Russian-language newspapers of trying to turn the population against Islam. The article contained a photograph of a grenade on top of the Quran. (Bureau on Human Rights and Rule of Law)

In the middle of May **Rustam Koshmuratov**, director of Radio Almaz (*Index* 3/1998), was ordered by the National Communications Agency (NAC) to sign a licence agreement obliging the station to report profits and expenses, the types of listener complaints and the services provided.

Under the agreement NAC would also have the right to require from the licensee any additional information that may be used to carry out routine and surprise inspections. Koshmuratov is refusing to sign the licence agreement because of the conditions. (Bureau on Human Rights and Rule of Law)

LATVIA

Lawmakers on 20 May voted by 52-1 to approve the principal amendment to the citizenship law, which would allow children born to non-Latvians after 21 August 1991 to become citizens at the age of 16, if they can demonstrate 'sufficient knowledge' of the language. (RFE/RL)

MALI

On the night of the 5 or 6 of May, **Cheick Oumar Konaré**, a journalist and director with the private daily *Sud-Info*, was attacked by assailants who claimed to be from the Adema Liberation Army. Konare was kidnapped by 10 men who interrogated him at length on the reasons for his opposition to the regime. He was then partially asphyxiated with gas and thrown with feet and hands bound into a ravine. His injuries were not serious. On 27 April, *Sud-Info* published an article on the recent resignations of seven high-ranking officers in the secret service. (RSF)

MALAYSIA

Opposition MP Lim Guan

Eng was sentenced to 18 months in jail after losing a 15 April appeal against convictions for sedition and publishing false information. In a 1995 pamphlet, Lim had questioned why a former state chief was not charged after a girl alleged he had raped her; for this, Lim was fined by the high court. But Judge Sri Gopal stated that a fine was too lenient, claiming that the judiciary's credibility had been attacked. Lim's custodial sentence will bar him from active politics. (*Far East Economic Review*)

Information Minister Mohamed Rahmat declared in late April that TV stations should not discuss the forest-fire haze affecting parts of Malaysia. Kuala Lumpur officials are concerned that repeated references to the problem will have a damaging effect on tourism. (*Far East Economic Review*)

MALAWI

Molland Nkhata, director of news at the state-controlled Malawi Broadcasting Corporation (MBC), was ordered on 23 April to retire from his position 'in the interest of the public'. In November 1997, he was demoted after reporting that President Bakili Muluzi had lost his voice at the Commonwealth Heads of Government summit in Scotland (*Index* 1/1998). After local and international outcry, Nkata was briefly reinstated to his original post. (MISA)

Police intend to sue the opposition *Daily Times*

newspaper and its editor **Charles Simango** for 'publishing unfounded, inaccurate, misleading and distorted stories about the police'. Inspector Oliver Soko told *New Vision* newspaper on 9 May that 'journalists have developed a tendency of writing false news articles which paint a bad image of the police.' The suit follows a *Daily Times* story which alleged that officers had misappropriated funds donated by an Asian group for community policing in Limbe, near Blantyre. (MISA)

Mabvuto Banda and **Chikumbutso Mtumodzi** of the *Daily Times* were subpoenaed on 25 May to testify for the state against opposition Malawi Congress Party MP **Hetherwick Ntaba**, who is being prosecuted for calling President Bakili Muluzi 'silly'. The *Daily Times* carried a story in which Ntaba also said: 'If Muluzi is a fool, he is a fool.' A group of plainclothes policemen later stormed into the offices of the *Daily Times* and interrogated reporters over the authenticity of the story. (MISA)

MAURITANIA

On 16 April the weekly *Actions* was censored without any explanation. The minister of the interior refused to turn over the proof of receipt to the editors, which meant they were not authorised to print that week's issue. Also on 16 April, the weekly *Nouakchott Infos* was seized in connection with an article published on serial rapes. (RSF)

The Arabic edition of the independent weekly *Le Calame* was censored on 4 May. Copies were held at the ministry of interior for a week and it was then declared that the issue would not be allowed to be sold on 30 April. The authorities have given no explanation for their actions. The Arabic version of weekly independent *La Tribune* was also censored without explanation on 29 May. (RSF)

MEXICO

On 12 April **Oriana Elicabe** and **Pascual Gorriz**, photographers from the Agence France Presse and Associated Press, were physically attacked by public security police at Tuxtla Gutierrez airport while taking pictures of a dozen foreigners leaving for Mexico City after being arrested and threatened with expulsion from Chiapas. They hit Gorriz, throwing him to the ground, and Elicabe was manhandled in a bid to confiscate their film. The attack was part of a campaign to prevent access by foreign journalists to the rebel state. (RSF)

On 17 May three armed individuals in a white van followed the chauffeur of journalist **Pablo Hiriart**, stopped his car and instructed him to tell his boss 'to stop publishing foolish remarks'. Hiriart is editor of the daily *La Cronica de Hoy* and, in recent months, has published stories implicating members of the government in drug trafficking. (RSF)

NICARAGUA

On 21 May President Arnoldo Alemán turned on journalists at a press conference after they questioned him about a narcotics scandal in which members of the government appear to be involved. The following day, Alemán insulted journalists again at a public event, calling them 'information terrorists'. (IFJ)

NIGER

Journalists have experienced higher levels of harassment since mid-April, in response to an opposition movement demanding the resignation of President Mainassara. On 15 April, several unidentified men surrounded the offices of the Nouvelle Imprimerie de Niger (NIP), a private printing house, and set it on fire. The offices were seriously damaged. On 18 April, while covering opposition demonstrations in Maradi, **Saadou Assane** of the daily *Le Républicain* was attacked by police and his equipment confiscated. He had to be hospitalised. A similar incident occured on 26 April when **Hassan Boukari**, a journalist with Ténéré FM – a station owned by the president's brother-in-law – was beaten by opposition militants at the headquarters of the Social Democratic Convention opposition party. Boukari also required hospitalisation. On 30 April, **Lawan Boucar,** a correspondent for Voice of America, evaded arrest by the presidential security squad after broadcasting an interview with the head of the Nigerien

Party for Democracy and Socialism. Meanwhile, managers of Radio et Musique, Anfani, Radio Souda and Ténéré FM were informed that no pro-opposition comments could be broadcast and managers were threatened by death should they disobey. (CPJ, RSF)

Moussa Tchangari, director of the independent weekly *Alternative*, was again arrested (*Index* 6/1997, 1/1998) on 4 May after reading out a statement on Radio Anfani condemning government attempts to silence the press. On 7 May, he was released without charge but, since then, the radio station has been silenced. Also on 7 May, **Mamane Abou**, owner of NIP and publisher of *Le Républicain* was arrested on suspicion of arson and insurance fraud. Meanwhile, **Soulwymane Keita** was arrested for broadcasting news of opposition demonstrations on the BBC. Police were also searching for **Ali Chekou**, editor of the independent weekly, *Le Citoyen*, after the paper published a statement by the independent press. By 20 May a total of 11 media outlets had been closed.(RSF, CPJ, BBC))

NIGERIA

Danlami Nmodu, Kaduna correspondent of *Tell,* was released on 6 April. Security agents interrogated him about the whereabouts of his editors, all of whom are currently either in hiding or detention. Nmodu was warned to refrain from writing stories deemed inflammatory by the State

Security Services (SSS). He was arrested on 27 March when security agents stormed his house at dawn. ('IPR')

On 20 April 50 SSS officers raided the editorial and administrative offices of the Independent Communication Network Ltd (ICNL), which publishes *News* magazine and *Tempo* and *PM* newspapers, arresting journalist **Austin Uganwa**, company accountant **Mufutau Lateef**, chief librarian **Anthony Nwana**, security officer **Borisanmi Olutuye**, special projects executive **Rotimi Obasa Osaba** and two other unnamed editorial staff. No charges were brought against the seven who were held at the Lagos headquarters of the Federal Intelligence and Investigations Bureau. On 23 April the agents returned and took away all ICNL computers. ('IPR')

Armed security agents on 20 April invaded the offices of the Independent Journalism Centre (IJC), arresting five staff members and punishing the rest by making them sit in the sun for three hours. Again no reasons were given for the subsequent ransacking except that the SSS wanted to know 'how the organisation continued when all its editors had either fled the country, or were in jail'. ('IPR', IJC)

Niran Malaolu, editor-in-chief of the *Diet* newspaper, was sentenced to life imprisonment on 28 April by the Special Military Tribunal for 'information gathering'. Malaolu was arrested on 28 December 1997 (*Index*

2/1998, 3/1998) and later charged in connection with a coup plot that the government claimed to have uncovered that month. In February, he and 26 other defendants were brought before the tribunal in a trial which was held *in camera* at a military barracks in Jos. Journalists were only allowed to attend on the opening and closing days. Amnesty said that Malaolu had been kept in solitary throughout his detention and had been denied to the right to choose independent defence lawyers. (AI, 'IPR')

On 30 April the government released 120 detainees including four journalists, after an amnesty announced by President Sani Abacha in November. The four include **Muhammed Adamu** and **Soji Omotunde**, from *African Concord* magazine, and **Onome Osifo-Whiskey**, managing editor of *Tell* (*Index* 5/1997, 1/1998). (IPR)

Kayode Akedire and **Femi Adefila,** journalists with the Oson state Broadcasting Corporation, were suspended indefinitely on 30 April for a report authorities said was offensive and embarrassing to the state government. The reporters had covered an ultimatum issued by the Nigeria Labour Congress on the issue of fuel shortages in the oil-rich state. ('IPR')

Three journalists with Ondo State Television Corporation were fired on 11 May. **Rotima Obamuwangun, Seinde Adeniyi** and **Ola Bamidele** are executive members of the station's chapter of the Nigeria

● ●

CYPRIAN EKWENSI

Re: My Son Amaechi Ekwensi – Deceased

To: General Officer Commanding
82 Division Nigerian Army
Enugu, Nigeria   25 May 1998

I am compelled to bring to your attention the painful death suffered by my son at the hands of the Nigerian Army stationed at Onitsha under your Command. Peter Amaechi Ekwensi, aged 32, was violently arrested on 10 April at Nkwelle-Ezunaka, our home village, by a patrol team in an Army Vehicle and conveyed to an unknown destination from which he will never return.

Meanwhile, unconfirmed information reached me that Amaechi was shot at close range inside the arresting vehicle; that profuse bleeding followed; and he was rushed to General Hospital Onitsha, then to Borromeo Hospital and finally to Toronto Hospital, Onitsha, before he was admitted, too late. The two military men who deposited the corpse were said to have paid for embalming and obtained a receipt. Is it then assumed that we must go and collect the dead body of our son – just like that? No explanation, no formalities. A human life, terminated abruptly.

We are seriously seeking your co-operation as follows:

1. Formal report of the death of Amaechi and the circumstances leading thereto, including post mortem.

2. Settlement of hospital bills where he was dumped.

3. Return of Amaechi's body to us in a respectable casket.

4. Funeral expenses for the burial.

5. Adequate compensation for members of his family but, above all else, the perpetrator(s) of this dreadful act must face the law of the land.

Amaechi was a small-scale industrialist, manufacturing *garri* from cassava and palm oil from palm fruit. He had been living in Nkwelle for some years and was supporting a staff of over a dozen youths who are now unemployed and in grief. He was a hero among the youths. He had committed no offence that deserved such brutality.

We request you give your immediate attention to this case. The family and the entire village are suffering greatly. They are in deep grief at the loss of their son, employer, friend and Master.

Chief Cyprian D. Ekwensi ❏

Cyprian Ekwensi is the author of numerous novels and short stories. His most recent, Jaqua Nana's Daughter, *was published in 1993 by Spectrum.*

● ●

WOLE SOYINKA

'Report only what you know'

There is no question in my mind that, if Chris Anyawu were standing here today, she would use the occasion to pay tribute to her comrades in the heat of the fray in that benighted nation called Nigeria. Next perhaps to their fellow practitioners in Algeria, I know of no other clan that has withstood such brutalisation as Nigerian journalists, yet continues to take the battle to their tormentors day after day, week after week, running the gauntlet of brutal repressions with ever-increasing ingenuity, both above and underground.

But we must also pay tribute to the endurance of their families, who have not been spared their own martyrdom in this increasingly deadly battle against the forces of darkness. Mindful of the example of Chris Anyawu, whose only crime was that she reported truthfully that there was no iota of truth in the earlier coup scenario that sent a former Head of State, General Olusegun Obasanjo and his own colleagues to long terms in prison. Colonel Ugbo, official spokesman for the Abacha junta, issued a familiar warning to Nigerian journalists – a familiar warning, yes, but one was now couched in a language that extended any prospective guilt of the journalistic trade beyond the actual practitioners. I quote him:

'"Report only what you know to save yourself and your family". Let me repeat that. "Report only what you know to save yourself and your family."'

With those words, the Abacha junta made official what, in any case, have become the commonplace practice of the enforcement agencies. A repugnant code in wartime – the practice of hostage-taking, the policy of guilt by association or accident of birth – this code of misconduct became publicly formalised. 'Report what you know', that is, 'report only what we tell you or we guarantee dire consequences not merely for you, the transgressor, but for your family – your husband or wife, your parent of grandparent, your sisters, brothers, cousins, even your infant children. Nigerians had finally arrived at the formal annunciation of fascism. ❑

This is an edited version of the introduction of a speech by acclaimed playwright **Wole Soyinka,** *given in London on 30 April to commemorate Press Freedom Day. Chris Anyawu was released from prison on 15 June.*

Union of Journalists. Their letters of dismissal from the Director of Finance and Administration said they were being dismissed for 'disloyalty and subversive activities against the government'. ('IPR')

Femi Adeoti, editor of the *Sunday Tribune*, was arraigned on 18 May before an Ibadan chief magistrate charged with 'rioting, arson and sedition'. He was detained on 6 May in connection with the lead story of the 3 May issue entitled 'Genesis of Ibadan Blood Bath', which reported the 1 May demonstrations in which seven people died in clashes with the police. He was granted bail on 4 June after over a month in detention. ('IPR')

SSS agents on 20 May raided the Lagos house of writer and democracy activist **Olubunmi Drum** in connection with the 1 May Ibadan riots. He was not at home so the agents threatened his wife. The family has since been forced into hiding. ('IPR')

On 25 May **Mosun Mosunro**, editor with Ogun State Television, was suspended indefinitely for authorising the broadcast of a press release item from the state's chapter of the Christian Association of Nigeria, which ordered its members to boycott prayers on the station. ('IPR')

On 15 June, **Chris Anyanwu**, publisher and editor of the now-defunct *Sunday Magazine*, was released from prison in an inaugural gesture by new head of state General Abdulsalam

Abubakar, having served nearly three years of a 15-year sentence for reporting an alleged coup plot in March 1995. Eight other prisoners were released, including General Olusegun Obasanjo, a former president, and human rights activist Dr Beko Ransome-Kuti. (*Financial Times, Guardian*, RSF, CPJ)

PAKISTAN

Catholic **Bishop John Joseph** shot himself in the head on 6 May in protest against a death sentence passed in April against **Ayub Masih**, who was convicted of defaming the Prophet Mohammed. During Joseph's burial service at Faisalabad cathedral on 10 May, 400 to 500 Muslim militants attacked a nearby village, called Christian Town, and demanded that law 295c, under which blasphemers can be executed, remain on the statute books. Christians have claimed for years that Muslims have used law 295c to extort money or land from members of minority faiths. (Reuters)

On 2 June anti-India protesters attacked a news conference called in Islamabad by the Pakistan-India People's Forum for Peace and Democracy (PIPFPD) to protest against nuclear tests by India and Pakistan in May. Members of the right-wing *Jamaat-i-Islami* and *Shabab-i-Milli* parties entered the hall and threw chairs at the PIPFPD members, who were already facing hostile questioning from reporters. (Reuters)

PALESTINE (AUTONOMOUS AREAS)

The Palestinian Authority ordered Reuters to close its Gaza office on 9 April after the news agency distributed a videotape that contained a statement from an alleged Hamas member. The man, who identifies himself on the tape as Adel Awadallah, accuses Jibril Rajoub, chief of preventive security, and other Palestinian security officials, of complicity in the killing of Muhyideen al-Sharif. Al-Sharif was the Hamas associate found dead next to an exploded car in Ramallah on 29 March. Palestinian Police Chief Ghazi Jebali said the office had been temporarily closed because it 'issued news that provoked sedition'. (CPJ)

Abbas al-Momani, a freelance cameraman working for a number of press organisations, was rearrested on 5 May – after a period of brief release since his initial arrest in mid-April – by General Intelligence and questioned about the same Hamas videotape, which has since been publicly broadcast by Reuters. Momani was released on 14 May. (A19)

PAPUA NEW GUINEA

Deputy Prime Minister Michael Nali, vexed over a critical editorial in the *National* newspaper, issued a threat to the foreign majority shareholders of the country's two daily newspapers. The *National* reported Nali on 15 April as saying that the right to free speech did not permit foreigners to participate in the country's 'political destiny'. In its editorial, the paper observed that Nali had commented publicly on issues beyond his remit since the prime minister was in the country. Though owned by a Malaysian company, the *National* has local shareholders. The *Post-Courier*, the island's other main daily, is mostly owned by Rupert Murdoch's News Corporation. (PINA)

PERU

On 7 April five people armed with revolvers and pistols assaulted Radio San Martin, carrying away transformers, recording and electrical equipment. (IFJ)

On 8 April journalist **Diogenes Torres Agreda**, host of a political programme on Radio Lima, was attacked with a pistol by Javier Kanashiro, mayor of the Lima district of San Martin de Porras. The mayor, who did not hit Torres, accused the journalist of ruining his political career. (IFJ)

On 13 April the pro-government daily *El Chino* published an 18-page supplement on **Gustavo Mohme**, opposition member of parliament and editor of the daily *La República*, accusing him of arms trafficking. The same charge has been brought against other members of the independent press, including **Baruch Ivcher** and **Edmundo Cruz** (*Index* 4/1997, 5/1997, 6/1996, 2/1998, 3/1998). (RSF)

Radio broadcaster **Gladys de**

la Cruz Pariona** was attacked on 9 April by two assailants in a minibus in the Victoria district of Lima. The journalist suffered multiple injuries and had her documents taken. De la Cruz was pursuing an intensive campaign on her programme *Solidaridad* in support of disabled people denied work opportunities. (IFJ)

Angel Paez, head of the Investigative Reporting Unit of *La República*, received a death threat from an unidentified source on 11 April. The incident occurred two days after a group of 12 men assassinated journalists **Isabel Chumpitaz Panta** and presenter **José Amaya Jacinto** (*Index* 3/1998). Paez is well known for her investigations into the wire-tapping of journalists and torture and assassinations by the Army Intelligence Service. (IFJ)

On 2 May an assistant editor working with **Miró Quesada Cisneros** of *El Comercio* newspaper (whose name was not made public) received a death threat on the eve of the publication of an interview with former police Captain Julio Salas. In the interview Salas accused presidential advisor Vladimiro Montesinos of having congratulated the police officers who were investigating Baruch Ivcher (*Index* 4/1997, 5/1997, 6/1997, 2/1998, 3/1998). Cisneros expressed particular concern since the death threat was made before the paper was published, implying its telephone lines are bugged. (RSF)

On 5 May **John Seclen**, a cameraman for *RTV-Jaen*, was detained by military authorities while leaving his workplace. The incident is thought to be connected with the criticism of the maltreatment of military recruits and their families exposed in the programme *Linea Directa*. (Instituto de Prensa y Sociedad)

On 7 May journalist **Carlos Paredes** and cameraman **Roger Córdova** of the ATV-Canal 9's *Sin Censura* were arrested for five hours in Chiclayo and accused of having committed offences against the security of the air force base near where they were found. The reporters had approached the base to interview a public relations official on the crash of a combat aircraft in which 74 people died. Their equipment was confiscated and their cassettes erased. (Instituto de Prensa y Sociedad)

Journalist **Cecilia Valenzuela**, host of the television programme *Here and Now* on Andina TV, received an anonymous death threat on 26 May. Valenzuela, whose programme includes debates and views opposed to the government, has been targeted since 1994, but had never before received a death threat. (Instituto de Prensa y Sociedad)

On 28 May members of the National Tax Supervision Administration went to the home of journalist **José Arrieta**'s wife to search for accounting documents and income statements from a company allegedly belonging to the former head of the Investigative Unit of Baruch Ivcher's Channel 2's *Frecuencia Latina* (*Index* 1/1998, 2/1998, 3/1998). Arrieta, who never owned a company, had already been charged twice with tax evasion and left the country in January. (Instituto de Prensa y Sociedad)

On 29 May *La República* published an article which claimed it had received documents which link the Arny Intelligence Service to attacks against journalists. The documents are mostly from the pro-government *El Tio*, which has run a sleaze campaign against individual *La República* journalists for several months . (Instituto de Prensa y Sociedad)

ROMANIA

On 7 May the government approved a draft law decriminalising homosexuality. The draft will revise the current penal code which deems homosexual relations punishable by a sentence of up to seven years, if they constitute a 'public offence'. RFE/RL)

RUSSIA

On 2 April **Ivan Fedyunin**, a reporter with *Bryanskie Izvestia,* was found stabbed to death in his apartment. His colleagues suggested his murder may have been connected to his articles concerning the alleged criminal activities of local companies involved in renovating apartments. (CPJ)

On 2 May Major **Igor Lykov** was shot twice at point blank range, in his apartment in Saratov, southeastern Moscow. (RFE/RL)

On 11 May it was reported that the military prosecutor for the Far East Region had renewed the imprisonment of **Grigory Pasko**. Prior to his arrest on 20 November 1997, after a trip to research the issues around soldiers killed and buried in Japan, Pasko worked for a navy newspaper *Boevaya Vakhta*, the Japanese daily *Asaki* and the TV channel NHK. He was accused of high treason after 'gathering state secrets in order to pass them to foreign organsations'. (RSF, HRW)

The Moscow Prosecutor's office announced on 13 May that no charges would be pressed against government officials who allegedly earned US$90,000 each for their joint authorship of a book chronicling the history of state privatisation. Among those paid was First Deputy Prime Minister Anatoly Chubais. Many commentators have suggested the payments were bribes to ensure the 'correct' version was told. (RFE/RL)

On 26 May NTV director-general Oleg Dobrodeev responded to President Yeltsin's charge that media owners were sometimes the 'worst censors'. In a statement to the world congress of the International Press Institute, he said the authorities were used to viewing television as a political weapon, and this had been reinforced by the 1996 presidential election coverage,

in which NTV openly supported Yeltsin's bid. Two days later, Yeltsin told top media executives that the state had no intention to restrict media freedom, but it did expect them to 'promote state policy'. (RFE/RL)

On 1 June the Moscow City Court overturned the lower court conviction of poet **Alina Vitukhnovskaya** on charges of drug possession with the intent to sell (*Index* 1/1996, 3/1998). The court found that Vitukhnovskaya's flat had been searched illegally and that this could not be used as a basis for her conviction. (RFE.RL)

On 2 June **Aleksei Ionov**, correspondent for *Volgodonskaya Nedelya Plus* based in Volgodonsk, was severely beaten near the editorial office by two assailants who threatened him with death if he continued to write articles against Mayor Sergey Gorbunov. (Alexander Zhabskiy)

On 8 June **Larissa Yudinka**, editor-in-chief of *Sovietskaya Kalmykia Segodnya*, the only independent newspaper in the Republic of Kalmykia, was killed. The Kalmykia government is suspected of involvement. (Glasnost Defence Foundation)

RWANDA

Former minister **Seth Sendashonga** was shot dead in Nairobi on the weekend of 9–10 May. His assassination has been linked to his denunciations of human rights violations by the present government and the security forces in Rwanda. (AI)

Rebels in the northwest are publicising their insurgency with a newspaper titled *Umucunguzi*, or Saviour. The publication urges people to take up arms against the 'army of occupation'. It accurately forecast the recent upsurge of fighting in Gitarma. (IRIN)

On 24 April 22 people were executed at five public locations in the first executions of those found guilty of participation in the genocide of 1994. None had access to defence lawyers, while some did not understand the trial procedures. The executions produced a flood of 2,000 confessions from other suspects in the hope of having their sentences reduced. Foreign Minister Anastase Gasana said it was 'one of the positive repercussions of the government's decision to carry out the death sentence'. (AI, IRIN)

SAMOA

On 15 May the government announced that top officials, from the prime minister to the heads of state corporations, may use public money to fund defamation suits against the media. The *Sunday Samoan* on 17 May called the policy 'an invitation to unchecked corruption'. The Journalists Association of Western Samoa noted that the policy was introduced while a decision is awaited in the Prime Minister Tofilau's defamation case against the *Samoa Observer* (*Index* 4/1997, 5/1997, 6/1997, 1/1998, 3/1998). (PINA)

The *Samoa Observer* will stop sending journalists to cover news conferences by the government's official spokesperson, the newspaper said on 21 May. **Savea Sano Malifa**, publishing editor of the *Samoa Observer*, called Deputy Prime Minister Tuilaepa Sailele Malilegaoi's news conferences 'an insufferable joke', adding 'it is not uncommon for him to belittle reporters who ask hard questions by saying they were out of line, or were inferior intellectually.' (PINA)

SENEGAL

On 16 May editor **Deissa Sall** and photographer **Cire Sow** of the Cameroon independent *Nouvel Horizon* were assaulted by militants in the home of Abdoulaye Diack, head of the Socialist Party in the Kaolack legislature of east Senegal. They were covering the electoral campaign in the region. Some US$4,000 worth of equipment was destroyed during the assault. (CPJ)

SERBIA-MONTENEGRO

On 21 April the authorities seized equipment and closed **TV Pirot** after President Milosevic and the relevant ministers expressed concern about the station's independent editorial policy. (B92, CPJ, ANEM)

Authorities closed border crossings into Kosovo to all private vehicles on 15 May, as state violence in the region escalated. Only vehicles of state-owned institutions have since been allowed to pass. Meanwhile, on 21 May, a group of armed Albanians wearing Kosovo Liberation Army (UCK) emblems detained a WTN television crew and a journalist of the Kyoto agency on the Prishtina-Pec road, forcing them to hand over their bullet proof vests. On 5 June the Pec-Djakovica road was seized by Serb police after a week long operation against the UCK. Journalists, diplomats and humanitarian workers have not been allowed to enter the area of operations. (RFE/RL, B92)

On 23 May shared broadcasts between Radio Television Serbia and Montenegrin Television were cut after journalist **Slavoljub Djukic** criticised the Belgrade authorities on air. Serbian director Dragoljub Milanovic made the decision after Djukic said on air, 'until the current regime in this country is changed, nothing good can be expected.' Montenegrin Television has promised to continue sending its signal to Belgrade 'for free, like always'. (RFE/RL)

Police beat dozens of men, women and children, protesting outside parliament on 25 May against the Bill on Universities, in one of the most brutal state interventions since the winter of 1996. The bill became law the following day and gave the government the power to appoint university rectors, deans of individual faculties and university boards of management. Academic staff claim the act destroys university autonomy. Two weeks later, the demonstrations were still continuing. On 2 June police confiscated the film of **Predrag Milosavljevic**, a reporter and photographer for the daily *Dnevni telegraf*, and **Milos Petrovic**, a Studio B cameraman. Both were covering the ongoing confrontation. (RFE/RL, RSF)

On 1 June Secretary Bozidar Jarevic denied accusations that the government had blocked the distribution of the *Politika* newspaper. Jarevic said that the government did not ban things and that 'it is common knowledge that Montenegro is an open and democratic society with freedom of information'. (B92)

SIERRA LEONE

Edward Smith, a stringer with the BBC World Service, was killed in an ambush in the village of Banbanduhun on 13 April. Smith, who had covered the north-eastern region of Sierra Leone for the BBC since the Armed Forces Ruling Council (AFRC) took power in May 1997, was travelling with West African ECOMOG soldiers in the Kono district when their vehicles were ambushed by junta forces. Smith previously worked as a reporter for the independent *Vision* newspaper and as editor of *Storm* for five years. (CPJ)

Five journalists were charged with treason at magistrate court in Freetown on 14 April. They were **Ibrahim Kargbo**, managing editor of the weekly independent *Citizen*; **Hilton Fyle**, managing director of WBIG FM and a former BBC

Network Africa Service presenter; Sierra Leone Broadcasting Services director, **Gipu Felix George**; on-air broadcaster **Denis Smith**; and newscaster **Olivia Mensah**, who is seven months pregnant. The latter also faces murder and spying charges. The charges are in connection with their alleged involvement in the 25 May 1997 coup, which overthrew the now re-instated president Tejan Kabbah. (CPJ)

On 31 April, Information Minister Julius Spencer accused journalists of *Punch* newspaper of collaborating with the ousted junta. The accusation was announced on radio and television in the wake of an article published on 29 April, headlined 'Guinea Refused to Hand Over AK Sesay'. Sesay was secretary to the chairman of the junta group. (CPJ)

SINGAPORE

The Ministry of Information and the Arts cancelled the publishing permit of the UK men's magazine *FHM* from 29 May because of its use of sexual images. The ministry said it has warned *FHM* but the magazine had not changed its style to satisfy local publishing standards. (Reuters)

Singnet, the country's largest internet provider, will launch Family-Online service in July which will block out pornographic websites. (Australian)

SOMALILAND

On 25 May **Hassan Said Yousuf**, chief editor of the

daily *Jamhuria*, was arrested by police for 'insulting important personalities, circulation of false information and criticising the leaders of the republic.' Yousuf was detained two days earlier, reportedly in connection with articles covering deteriorating relations between army and government; the existence of Rift Valley Fever; the punitive amputations ordered by an Islamic court on 33 people; and 'insults' against the prosecutor general and members of the judiciary. (RSF)

SOUTH AFRICA

Madeleine Van Biljon, a well-known Afrikaner writer who won a special award from the Afrikaans Language and Culture Association (ATKV), had the prize withdrawn on 7 May on the grounds that it was 'only for Christians'. ATKV was set up as a cultural arm of the Afrikaner Broederbond, the secret political mafia behind the *apartheid* National Party government. During a recent interview with *Finesse*, a magazine aimed at Christian women, Van Biljon had said that she was a non-believer. (*Southern Africa Report*)

During Truth Commission hearings into South Africa's chemical and biological warfare programme on June 11th, Daan Goosen, managing director of Roodeplaat Research Laboratory, a front company for the military, described the anonymous offer of a 'race-specific' bacterium made in 1983 or 1984. Goosen said a document delivered to the South African embassy in

London stated that the bacterium 'has only got the possiblity of making sick and killing pigmented people'. Wouter Basson, head of chemical and biological warfare programme, was instructed to take up the offer, but the mission was aborted for fear it was a trap. The commission was also supplied with enough LSD to incapacitate 50,000 people, 100,000 to 200,000 mandrax sedative tablets and 200 kilograms of marijuana to be used in 'riot control'. (*Guardian*)

SOUTH KOREA

The ruling National Congress for New Politics decided on 20 April to allow foreign corporations access to the satellite and television industries. It also agreed to end pre-censorship of film dramas, cartoons, commercial programs and imported television products. (*Korea Herald*)

Son Chung Mu, publisher of *Inside the World* magazine, was arrested on 1 June on charges of defamation and for accepting money from the former chief of the Korean CIA, Kwon Young Hae, to slander the then presidential candidate Kim Dae Jung during the 1997 election campaign. Two other journalists, **Chon Bong Jae**, publisher of *World Korea*. and **Ham Yun Shik** of *One Way* magazine, face similar charges. (CPJ)

Recent publication: *Long term prisoners still held under the National Security Law* (AI, May 1998); *On trial for defending his rights: the case of the human rights activist Suh Jun-sik* (AI, May 1998)

SPAIN

Retired Col. Amadeo Martinez Inglés admitted on 2 May that he had known since 1981 about the Argentinian 'death flights', in which dissidents were thrown out of planes into the sea. Ingles' comments were made to Buenos Aires' Radio Mitre and confirm evidence given to Judge Baltasar Garzón, who is conducting an enquiry to clarify responsibility for the deaths of 600 Spanish passport-holders in Argentina during the 1973 to 1986 dictatorship. (Associated Press)

On 19 May death threats against TV journalists **Mercedes Milá** of Antena 3 and **José María Calleja** of Canal Plus were painted on the wall of a cultural centre in San Sebastian. No one has claimed responsibility for the graffiti. (RSF)

The trial of former interior minister Jose Barrionuevo and 11 others began in Madrid on 25 May. Barrionuevo is accused of involvement with the GAL anti-terrorist group, set up in 1983 to counter the Basque separatist ETA. GAL is suspected of killing at least 27 ETA sympathisers between 1983 and 1987. The existence of the 'secret army' was concealed by the Socialist administration. (*European, Guardian, International Herald Tribune*)

SRI LANKA

On 5 May the human rights agency Peace Brigades International (PBI) stated that it had been forced to leave the country because of the government's demand to be allowed to 'edit' the organisation's reports. The authorities also demanded that PBI provide them with a list of all its clients and contacts. (Peace Brigades International, Reuters, *Hindu, Sri Lanka Monitor*)

Police arrested two air force officers on 5 May over an attack on *Sunday Times* defence columnist **Iqbal Atthas** (*Index* 2/98) last February. The men had been responsible for the security of the then commander of the airforce, Oliver Ranasinghe, who Atthas claims was behind the attack. The two accused were released on bail on 8 May, and are scheduled to appear in court on 10 June. (Reuters, AI)

For the third time since September 1995 (*Index* 6/1996, 3/1996, 1/1996, 6/1995), the government imposed censorship on all military-related news on 5 June. A defence ministry press statement said that print and electronic media were prohibited from carrying news about operations by the military, police and the para-military special task force, and that Major General J. Nammuni, deputy chief of staff of the army, had been appointed the 'competent authority' to implement the regulations. (Reuters)

• •

SUNANDA DESHAPRIYA

Blackout

The Free Media Movement (FMM) vehemently condemns the imposition of Emergency (Prohibition on Publication and Transmission of Sensitive Military Information) Regulation No. 1 of 1998, which was promulgated on 5 June 1998, as a grave violation of the basic rights of the people of Sri Lanka. The FMM is equally concerned about the fact that, for the first time, the sole responsibility for censoring military news has been given to a military officer, breaking with the democratic tradition of civilian control over the military.

On two occasions in the past years – in September 1995 and in April 1996 – when the government imposed censorship of military news, the consequences were quite negative. There was also no advantage for the troops on the battlefront at the time. It was conclusively proved that censorship of military news could not prevent the people from getting to known about the losses and setbacks suffered by the military in the course of the conflict. The FMM believes that the imposition of censorship is aimed at preventing the media from reporting the truth about the war to the people of this country. Therefore, it is obvious that this is more a part of a political strategy than a military requirement.

It is already clear that censorship of military news is aimed at making only the state version and pronouncements about the war available to the people. This censorship will prohibit accurate reporting of whatever discussions on the ethnic conflict take place during the forthcoming election campaign for the Provincial Councils. The FMM strongly feels that this would restrict the ability of the people to make an informed choice at the elections.

Therefore, the FMM calls upon the government to withdraw the Emergency Regulation that has imposed censorship of military news.❏

Sunanda Deshapriya is secretary-general of the Free Media Movement

• •

TAJIKISTAN

In late May parliament passed a law banning religious parties which effectively prevents the Islamic opposition from contesting the elections due to be held later this year. President Rahmonov said there was no choice but to ban religious parties since the country is a secular state. (SWB)

TANZANIA

On 11 April police briefly detained and interrogated **Balinagwe Mwambungu**, managing editor of *Mfanyakazi* newspaper which, on that day, had published a story suggesting that the ruling CCM party was 'wayward' in addressing the issue of Muslim riots in a Dar es Salaam mosque. (MISA)

Peter Sambara, a reporter with *Majira* newspaper, was detained on 15 April in connection with an article claiming that police had forced civilians to help them search for the bodies of miners killed in a recent disaster. (MISA)

On 16 April **Kiondo Mshana**, editor of Kiswahili paper *Taifa Letu*, was detained by police wanting to know the name of the writer of a story which had quoted detained Islamic leader, Sheikh Magezi. Mshana refused to answer. (MISA)

On 3 June, *Mtanzania* photojournalist **Ally Mwankufi** was beaten by police after taking photos of suspects being arrested at Kinondoni Mkwajuni after a murder. (MISA)

On 8 June, the government banned three Kiswahili weekly tabloids - *Kasheshe, Chombeza* and *Arusha Leo* - due to what it called their 'persistent featuring of pornographic cartoons'. (MISA)

TRINIDAD AND TOBAGO

Barbadian-born TV journalist **Julian Rogers** was denied the renewal of his work permit on 30 April for 'broadcasting testimonies by people who do not support the government'. (AMARC)

TURKEY

On 21 April police forced journalists to leave a courtroom in Aydin, where officers were on trial for torturing to death student **Baki Erdogan** in 1993. Outside the courthouse, five of them were beaten up: **Mert Ilkutlug** of *Milliyet*; **Hakan Gulce** of ATV; columnist **Celal Baslangic**; and *Radikal* journalists **Selma Yildiz** and **Ahmet Sik**. Several others received hospital treatment after being detained. In May six officers were found guilty of killing **Baki Erdogan**. (RSF)

It was reported on 28 April that journalist **Mehmet Ali Birand** had been sacked from *Sabah* newspaper after reports that a captured Kurdish rebel commander had accused him of links to separatist guerrillas (*Index* 3/98). He called the allegation 'ridiculous'. (Reuters)

President of Turkey's Human Rights Association **Akin Birdal** survived an assassination attempt on 12 May when gunmen shot him six times at close range. Birdal faces a stream of charges for his outspoken criticism of Turkey's human rights performance and treatment of its Kurdish minority. (AI, HRW, Reuters, *Turkish Daily News*)

On 24 May journalist **Adnan Gerger**, of private TV chain ATV, was attacked by unknown individuals who repeatedly hit him on his face and warned of the consequences of his writing. Gerger was investigating the attempted murder of Akin Birdal, president of the Turkish Human Rights Association. (RSF)

On 27 May **Mehmet Sanli Ekin**, journalist with the pro-Kurdish newspaper *Ulkede Gundem*, was detained by Istanbul's anti-terror division. He was visiting the Security Office to get an extension on his passport when he was taken into custody, on the apparent order of security forces in the southeast. *Ulkede Gundem* was closed down for 10 days in May for publishing an article by a jailed Kurdish parliamentarian. (RSF)

On 31 May, the Higher Education Board (YOK) quietly amended its regulations to allow the expulsion of university students involved in 'incidents', even if they take place off campus. This means that students demonstrating against the 'headscarf ban' could be expelled. (*Sabah*)

On 1 June playwright **Esber Yagmurdereli**, who had been in hiding since January, was arrested and sent back to a prison in Ankara on the grounds that he had violated the release condition that he not 're-offend' (*Index* 2/1998). Yagmurdereli is now expected to serve the remainder of his original 16-year sentence, as well as a fresh 10-month term for the new conviction. (PEN)

A teenager was given a 10-month suspended sentence on 2 June for comments he made on the Internet. **Emre Ersoz** was charged with publicly insulting state security forces after being reported to the police by another internet user and traced via the provider, Turknet. Ersoz had taken part in a debate centred around police treatment of a group of blind people protesting against potholes in Ankara's pavements. (Reuters)

It was reported on 9 June that the European Court of Human Rights had upheld the case of Kurdish journalist **Salih Tekin**, from the daily *Ozgur Gundem,* who was arrested and tortured by police in 1993, saying the facts had been established beyond reasonable doubt. (Reuters)

On 16 June Turkish journalist **Ragip Duran**, formerly of the BBC and AP, gave himself up to the state prosecutor to serve out a sentence imposed in 1994. He was charged for an article in the banned daily *Ozgur Gundem* about the PKK. (RSF)

TURKMENISTAN

On 17 April opposition leader **Abdy Kuliyev** was arrested at Ashgabat airport after returning from five years of exile. He is being held under house arrest and has reportedly been charged with trying to overthrow the government. The same day, **Muhammet Berdiyev**, a stringer for Radio Liberty's Turkmen service covering Kuliev's arrival, was forbidden by the authorities to go to the airport within minutes of having been given the assignment. On 20 April **Dudymurad Khodzha-Mukhammed** was released after being held in a psychiatric hospital since February 1996. (AI, CPJ)

UGANDA

In early May the East Africa Media Institute moved its secretariat from Nairobi to Kampala, after waiting for over 18 months for the Kenyan government to register it. The organisation complained of the lack of commitment on the part of Kenyan journalists to establish a local chapter. (NDIMA)

Police began investigating the Central Broadcasting Station (CBS) at the beginning of June over *Ekijja Omanyia,* a radio programme focussing on the controversial draft Land Bill. CBS has been publically criticised by President Museveni for 'inciting the public to rise against the constitution' over the bill. On 2 June the shows' host, **Mulindwa Muwonge**, was interrogated for four hours by

the Criminal Investigations Department. He was accused of uttering 'dangerous' remarks about the Land Bill during his transmission on 31 May. (*Monitor, New Vision*)

UNITED KINGDOM

It was decided in early May that *The Sunday Times* writer A. A. Gill would not be charged with incitement to racial hatred. Gill had described the Welsh as 'loquacious dissemblers, immoral liars, stunted, bigoted, dark, ugly, pugnacious little trolls' in an article. (*Independent*)

Secretary of State for Culture, Media and Sport Chris Smith took a stand against Rupert Murdoch's BSkyB satellite broadcaster in early June. Smith informed the EC that Murdoch's stations were failing to comply with the 1989 EU directive 'Television without Frontiers', under which one tenth of programming must be produced by independent European companies. None of the BskyB channels were found to be achieving this target. (*Guardian, Telegraph*)

In early June Conservative MP Alan Duncan announced that he would cut a chapter from the paperback edition of his political work, *Saturn's Children.* Duncan was recently appointed to the Conservative front bench as a health spokesman. The section he removed called for the legalisation of drugs. Duncan claimed that the decision was taken before he knew of the new job. (*Guardian*)

SUNNY OZIDEDE

Asylum, perjury and video

Iam an Ogoni and was a student activist in the protests against Shell's destruction of our lands. I was arrested, imprisoned and tortured three times and finally fled in 1996. My claim for asylum was refused by the UK Home Office.

They put me in Campsfield and tried to deport me. After the protest, the Campsfield Nine Defence Campaign got me better lawyers and sent a doctor to Bullingdon, who confirmed that what I had said about my torture was true. At my appeal hearing, the adjudicator accepted that the Home Office had been wrong.

In the early morning of 20 August 1997 Group 4 private security guards came for two detainees because they had 'complained' the day before. We all woke up when we heard one of them screaming: we thought he was being strangled. In court, my barrister showed a clip from a Group 4 surveillance cameras, which showed a guard with two hands around his neck. Supervisor John Allen admitted 'it was not done by the book'.

Group 4 told so many lies in court. Caryn Mitchell-Hill said I had taken her by the shoulders and threatened her: the videos showed her in a different place. She refused to identify herself (on the video) and her boyfriend Chris Barry, another Group 4 guard, also refused to identify her, even though it was obviously her. Barry claimed he had been 'concussed', kicked and punched, his shirt torn and a bottle of chemicals poured over him by me; the video show him walking along with a clean dry shirt.

We think Group 4 did most of the damage the Home Office minister, keeps talking about. Guards Mo Stone and Terry Morley even admitted they had smashed a telephone 'to stop (us) communicating with the outside world'. ❏

Sunny Ozidede is one of the nine West African asylum seekers charged with riot at Campsfield Immigration Detention Centre on 20 August 1997. They were cleared on 17 June 1998, after the 15th Group 4 witness introduced another false allegation. Sunny won refugee status and was released on bail in April 1998. But five not on bail were immediately taken back into Immigration custody and are threatened with instant deportation. No Group 4 guard has been charged with perjury. Sunny was interviewed by **Theresa Hayter**

On 3 June Prime Minister Tony Blair denied that 170kg of uranium had gone missing from Dounreay nuclear power station in the late 1960s. Both Blair and nuclear industry officials attribute the apparent disappearance to an 'accounting error'. Scottish National Party leader Alex Salmond had claimed that enough uranium had gone missing to manufacture 12 atomic bombs. (*Guardian, Independent, Telegraph*)

Garry Thomas, assistant editor of *Climber* magazine, was awarded £10,000 compensation for unfair dismissal by an industrial tribunal on 3 June. He had printed a photograph of a decomposing body in an effort to make the magazine 'more exciting'. (*Telegraph*)

The third edition of William St Clair's *Lord Elgin and the Marbles* was published on 8 June. The author claims that, in the late 1930s, the Marbles were irreparably damaged when scrubbed with metal scrapers. The museum denies suppressing the facts surrounding this incident. In 1994, St Clair was denied access to British Museum records. (*Guardian*)

URUGUAY

On 27 May **Carlos Ardaix**, journalist with Radio Tabare de Salto, was given a five-month, suspended prison sentence for defaming a doctor at Salto hospital during a live transmission of his programme *Nuestra Gente*. Ardarix had read out a letter, written by the brother of a young woman whose baby had died while in labour, which accused the obstetrician of contributing to the death of the baby. The judge said that the broadcast could damage the obstetrician's reputation. (RSF)

USA

National Public Radio editor and journalist Larry Matthews has been charged by Maryland prosecutors with nine counts of possession and six counts of distribution of child pornography. Matthews is claiming a defence under the First Amendment, saying he was researching a story on internet child pornography and attempts to police it when he was arrested. Matthews claims he had no success approaching people in child pornography 'chat rooms' as a journalist, so he took on the persona of the type of person he wanted to contact. He received several photos as a result of the tactic and, in hope of gaining the trust of a contact, he sent some photos over the web. That's when the police arrested him. The case, set to come before the court in July, will be the first involving the Internet and child pornography, and may set a precedent in dictating which dangerous subjects journalists can or cannot research. 'It's a frightening thing.' said Matthews. 'Can the government take any topic and say, the only thing you're allowed to report is what we tell you?' (*Guardian*)

Dictionary publisher Merriam-Webster has rejected demands that they leave the word 'nigger' out of their dictionaries in the future. Many groups such as the National Association for the Advancement of Colored People want the word dropped, but the 150-year-old publisher said in early May it will do no more than add a note in italics to denote words that are racial, religious or sexual slurs. 'As long as the word is in use, it is our responsibility to put it in the dictionary,' a spokesman said. (*The Times*)

America OnLine (AOL), the world's largest internet service provider with 14 million customers, adopted a new privacy policy on 3 June in the face of a government report condemning the state of online privacy. A Federal Trade Commission (FTC) report released on 4 June said that hundreds of companies on the internet are collecting information about people and their web-browsing habits, and selling the data. The FTC spent a year surveying data collection at 1,400 World Wide Web sites, and found that companies also collect information on children's internet habits. AOL's new policy gives customers the right to limit sale of their information, and forbids the collection of children's information without the permission of the parent. (Reuters)

Recent publication: *From San Diego to Brownsville: Human rights violations on the USA-Mexico border* (AI, May 1998)

US VIRGIN ISLANDS

The former editor of the *Virgin Islands Daily News* filed a lawsuit against the newspaper's owner on 5 June, claiming she was illegally pressured to resign in May. **Penny Feuerzeig** was demoted from editor to editorial page editor after the paper's sale by Gannett Newspapers to Jerry Prosser on 5 January. Feuerzeig, granted autonomy over the page's content, was then forced to send all copy to the new editor of the *Daily News* for approval. She resigned on 29 May in the midst of a controversy over an editorial Prosser wrote in support of the Virgin Islands Telephone Corporation, which he also owns. Feuerzeig claims in her suit that Prosser reneged on pension plans, violated workplace agreements and defrauded her. The *Daily News* won a Pulitzer Prize for investigative reporting while she was editor. (Reuters)

VIETNAM

Nguyen Tung Chi, editor of *Tien Phong* (Avant-Garde), a newspaper for young people, was attacked and beaten on 16 April. The journalist was in a restaurant when he was set upon by six to eight men who tried to put out his eyes with a broken beer bottle. The attackers also stole a bag which contained Nguyen's documents. (RSF)

YEMEN

On 7 June a San'aa Court ordered the release of a three-member BBC film crew arrested on 26 May for violating Yemen's press laws while filming in a remote region without permission. The BBC regional correspondent **Rageh Omaar**, producer **Robin Barnwell** and cameraman **Frank Smith** were covering the recent story of a British family kidnapped and held by Bani Dhabyan tribesmen for three weeks. (*The Times*)

ZAMBIA

Joy Sata, a reporter with the state-owned *Zambia Daily Mail*, was threatened with disciplinary action for condemning the newspaper's editorial practice of censoring stories critical of government. She made the comments on a TV programme on 4 May. (MISA)

On 19 May, the government obtained an *ex-parte* injunction barring the privately owned daily *Post* from publishing statements made by state witnesses, due to testify in the October 1997 coup attempt trial which began on 1 June *Index* 1/1998, 2/1998, 3/1998). Under a story headlined 'State Has Evidence Problems', the *Post* had reported on 19 May that witness statements to police were insufficient to secure a conviction. (MISA)

On 27 May a Lusaka court convicted Chinese national **Xiang Rong** for possessing pornographic materials and fined her US$840. Her lawyer, Michael Musonda, said Rong was found in possession of pornographic magazines and a video which she bought at a stand in South Africa. Under Zambian law its is an offence to be found in possession of 'obscene writings, drawings, prints, paintings, printed matter, pictures posters, emblems, photographs, videos or any other object tending to corrupt morals'. (MISA)

The Lusaka High Court limited the number of journalists covering the 1 June treason trial to only one from a selected list of local and international news organisations. They will be allowed to cover the treason trial stemming from the October 1997 coup attempt. Court administrator Philip Musonda blamed the restriction on lack of space. (MISA)

Former vice-president Godfrey Miyanda on 3 June withdrew criminal libel charges against the *Post*, preferring to pursue a civil libel action against the newspaper and its former special projects editor, **Masautso Phiri**. He sued the paper in December 1996, for an article headed 'Praising God Loudly', which he claimed ridiculed him and suggested he was not fit for office. (MISA)

Compiled by: Lucy Hiller, Regina Jere-Malanda, Suzanne Fisher (Africa); Andrew Kendle, Melissa Ong, Nicky Winstanley-Torode (Asia); Simon Martin (eastern Europe and CIS); Dolores Cortés (south and central America); Arif Azad, Rupert Clayton, Gill Newsham, M.Siraj Sait (Middle East); Andrew Elkin, Suzanne Fisher (north America and Pacific); and Andrew Blick (UK and western Europe).

Tehran Spring

It's not all football. Things are stirring inside Iran as well as on the terraces of the World Cup. *Index* rifles through the pages of the Iranian press to glimpse what's going on

*File compiled and translated by Nilou Mobasser.
Also with the help of Florida Safiri*

FARAJ SARKOOHI

Showdown

Iran's new President, Mohamad Khatami, campaigned on a free expression platform and came to power in a surprise election victory on 23 May last year with an overwhelming mandate from the people. The press, writers and artists – as well as the 70 per cent of the population under 20 – breathed deep of the air of freedom that swept through the stifling atmosphere of the fundamentalist regime. On the first anniversary of Khatami's election, the regime struck back, seeking once again to stifle debate – and to regain control of the country's future

The fundamentalist-controlled General Court of Tehran ruled on 10 June to close down *Jameah* – a daily that began publication only six months ago and already has a circulation of 400,000 – on the grounds that it had, among other offences, revealed state secrets. The charge was made by Major General Rahim Safavi, chief commander of the Iranian Revolutionary Guards.

The proprietor of *Jameah* was barred for 12 months from taking part in any media activity; the court also ordered the closure of the weekly *Panjshanbeha* (Thursdays).

Jameah's representatives have protested against the court ruling and the newspaper's chief editor, Mashallah Shamsolvaezin, announced that publication would continue for 21 days pending an appeal hearing.

The publisher of the second daily in disfavour, *Gozaresh Rooz*, (Daily Reporter) announced that publication would cease following the misconduct warning from the Ministry of Islamic Guidance and Culture (*Ershad*).

The moves against the three papers demonstrated the ruling

fundamentalist's desire to curb even the limited press freedom that exists in my country. The attacks on the press are in keeping other repressive moves by the Islamic regime in recent months. These include:

● the arrest and trial of Tehran's influential mayor, Gholamhoseyn Karbashi, a member of the religious intelligentsia supporting President Khatami;

● attacks on Grand Ayatollah Montazeri, a leading figure in the Iranian clergy who has directly criticized head of state Ayatollah Khamene'i, and his followers;

● repression of workers' strikes and suburban uprisings;

● rejection of all applications for the founding of non-governmental organisations like political parties, trade unions, writers' and press associations, women's organizations etc.

The reluctance of the Islamic regime to accept any reforms, however limited, is also shown by its refusal to honour Khatami's election pledge to release political prisoners and prisoners of conscience. Further, it has continued with the use of censorship, torture and the practice of stoning dissidents to death via the 'revolutionary courts' of which it retains control.

The fundamentalists, who dominate the regime and the *majlis*, appear increasingly desperate in the face of popular support for a move towards democracy. A month ago, Major General Safavi told a summit meeting of fellow-commanders that the current situation was intolerable and declared that the Revolutionary Guard was ready to 'cut out the tongues and sever the necks' of all critics and opponents of the Islamic regime. The speech was published by *Jameah* and other papers, and aroused widespread criticism, partly on the grounds that the Constitution forbade the Revolutionary Guard from involving itself in politics, partly because the speech showed that the regime was not prepared to listen to the pro-democracy forces in Iran.

At present, there are three clearly definable tendencies in Iranian politics:

● the fundamentalist-royalist faction supporting a totalitarian political structure;

● a faction with a more moderate and liberal interpretation of Islamic principles (the 'Khatami wing');

● the faction supporting freedom and democracy that unites socialists, social democrats, secularists, liberals and most of the Iranian

jameah
Damned, but still on the streets

Among the official charges lodged against *Jameah* newspaper were:

● 'Slander and insults'; complaint lodged by Rahim Safavi, Islamic Revolution Guards Corps commander.
● 'Publishing falsehoods and creating public anxiety'; complaint lodged by Rahim Safavi and Mohsen Rafiqdust, the head of the Foundation for the Underprivileged and Disabled, and the director-general for judicial affairs of the Prisons Organisation and the head of Tehran's justice department.
● 'Publishing material and photographs transgressing public decency'; complaint lodged on behalf of the public.

The accused was exonerated of all other charges, including a complaint by the joint staff headquarters of the Islamic Revolution Guards Corps accusing *Jameah* of 'publishing news about confidential matters' – aka breaking the official secrets act. The paper's publisher is appealing against the paper's banning and it continues to appear in even more flamboyant style pending the appeal hearing in July.

intelligentsia.

Jameah supports the second faction. Its role in extending freedom of the press is an important one, as its popularity stems from the fact that more than any other journal it has reflected criticism of the regime as well as different viewpoints in Iranian society. It also supported Mayor Karbaschi against his accusers. At first, the paper had the support of culture minister Ataollah Mohajerani; however, two weeks ago, he accused it of extremism, a move seen by critics as a retreat by Khatami under pressure from the fundamentalists.

The trial of Tehran's mayor and the press crackdown have convinced many people that the President does not have the power to implement his promised reforms of the Islamic regime.

Throughout this century, the people of Iran have made repeated bids for freedom and democracy: first in the Constitutional Revolution of 1905, then in the movement to nationalize the Iranian oil industry in 1951 and again in 1979, in the revolution that overthrew the Shah. Each time, popular participation in the political scene has been ultimately suppressed by dictatorial rule. The past two decades under harsh totalitarian regimes have taught the Iranian people that economic, social and cultural development are impossible without democracy.

In the absence of political parties, trade unions and the like, the press and literature have become the sole means by which the voices of the people can be heard. The court move to close down *Jameah* is one link in a planned chain of events – a step by step coup d'état being staged by the fundamentalists. The fate of *Jameah* and of the Mayor of Tehran may be decided in the weeks to come; the Iranian people's struggle for freedom and democracy will not be so easily put down. ❏

Faraj Sarkoohi, an Iranian writer and journalist is currently in Sweden. He wrote this piece for the Swedish daily Dagens Nyheter

The Iranian press

The following sampler from the Iranian press reflects its wide range of debate and new freedom to comment and criticise

Iranian newspapers reflect a wide range of positions on a variety of issues. It is therefore difficult to summarise each paper's stance in a single word or phrase. There is no given 'package' of issues espoused in all its aspects by a given paper. On the economy, for example, a paper may be – to varying degrees – pro-market [*Ettela'at*] or pro-state planning [*Salam*]; on foreign policy, they can be isolationist and anti-western [*Jomhuri-ye Eslami*] or in favour of improved foreign relations [Iran]; on social issues they can favour restrictiveness [*Kayhan*] or promote openness [*Hamshahri*]; in terms of political affiliation, they can be very pro-Khatami [*Jameah*] or very anti-Khatami [*Resalat*]. The important and striking thing about Iran's press today is the ferment of ideas and its uninhibited engagement with issues.

However, to give the uninitiated reader a general impression, below is a list roughly reflecting the position of Iran's major Persian-language dailies rated on their commitment to freedom of expression on a scale of 1-12, with 1 as the most active supporter of greater pluralism and 12 its most virulent opponent. Numbers 1 to 7 are definitely on the side of greater freedom of expression, undoubtedly a reflection of the views of a nation that voted three to one in favour of President Mohammad Khatami.

1. *Jameah* [Society]
2. *Salam* [Hello]
3. *Iran*
4. *Hamshahri* [Fellow citizen]
5. *Kar va Kargar* [Work and Worker]
6. *Ettela'at* [Information]
7. *Akhbar* [News]
8. *Abrar* [The Pious]

9. *Farda* [Tomorrow]
10. *Jomhuri-ye Eslami* [Islamic Republic]
11. *Resalat* [Mission]
12. *Kayhan* [World]

Iran also boasts a burgeoning number of weeklies, monthlies and 'occasionalies'. These no doubt have smaller circulation figures, but they have the advantage of being able to explore issues in greater depth. Notable among these are the monthly *Kiyan*, which regularly publishes material by Abdolkarim Sorush; *Iran-e Farda*, associated with the Freedom Movement of Iran, formerly led by Mehdi Bazargan and currently by Ebrahim Yazdi; and *Zanan*, the monthly focusing on women's issues. ❑

'By the almighty pen' — jameah

MASHALLAH SHAMSOLVAEZIN

Today, we present the newspaper's fiftieth issue to our honourable readers. Since 5 February 1998 [the first issue], *Jameah* has experienced many ups and downs. On the whole, and in the light of the unprecedented enthusiasm shown by our audience and our country's political and social circles, these ups and downs have, on the one hand, filled the people running *Jameah* with pride and, on the other hand, increased and intensified their responsibilities. And, of course, this is only the beginning of the road: a difficult but emboldening road; a road with many twists and turns but one that is character-building; a road never travelled but not one that leads nowhere.

We make no claims to perfection as we travel this road, nor do we consider ourselves immune from erring or making mistakes. Easily and confidently, we share everything that is happening around us with our audience, daily strengthening the bridge of confidence created in this way.

During the last few weeks, many questions have been directed at us regarding some of the newspaper's contents. In particular, with the increase in the material in the newspaper criticising the paper itself, readers have reacted in two different ways. The first group is of the opinion that the people running *Jameah* and the editor-in-chief in particular are under pressure to do this. The second believes this is a new method of reducing pressure being skilfully deployed by the people running *Jameah*. The frank and transparent answer is that this behaviour is a proper part of the newspaper's natural course in the process of propagating a culture that accepts different points of view and tendencies. The people running *Jameah* are thinking about the auspicious outcome of such behaviour in national terms.

In this fiftieth issue, *Jameah* will reiterate its 10 principles for the benefit of new readers and as a sign of its commitment to abide by them.

We expect the honourable readers of *Jameah* – who are its real owners – to maintain their shrewd vigilance in their supervision of the performance of their chosen newspaper. *Jameah* is thinking about the future.

'By the almighty pen,

'*Jameah* newspaper, the first issue of which lies before its honourable readers, intends – by the grace of God and in view of the auspicious times we are experiencing and in the light of its journalistic responsibilities – to strive towards the establishment of civil society in Iran.

'Civil society is a model of one kind of collective life that has been experienced in today's advanced societies, bringing amazing gains for the nations who have opted for this model.

'Notwithstanding the varying views on its origins, standard bearers and the ideal environment for its birth, on 2nd Khordad [23 May 1997 presidential election that brought Khatami to power] it [the notion of civil society] emerged for the first time from its limited theoretical framework among intellectuals, was transformed by President Khatami into something that could be discussed at a national level and rapidly turned into a near collective wish in our country. In a word, civil society means giving official recognition to the rights of citizens and placing their rights above their duties within a defined framework which, today, despite the existence of a national covenant [the Constitution] and the passage of 19 years since the Islamic revolution, has taken an unequal and mainly one-sided course to the advantage of the state and the government. However, without a doubt, realising this concept in a society with the characteristics of Iranian society is a task that requires much work. And mass media, especially the written media, can play a role in guiding public culture towards an ideal society while still safeguarding the people's national and religious identity. *Jameah* is the first example in the press to be founded on the concept of civil society. It has directed its gaze towards a future in which the press has found its true position and rank – in a brave and proud society – as 'the fourth estate'.

'The principles that are laid out below for the attention of our honourable readers are in effect the charter of a new journalistic institution, displayed in a frank and transparent way for the benefit of its audience:

● 1 *Jameah* is, first and foremost, a professional newspaper that strives to perform its duty within the framework of the Press Law and with respect for honest news reporting, without judgement or pre-judgement.

● 2 *Jameah* has ensured that all its material carries bylines. This is out of respect for the creator of the work and in order to train a responsible and bold journalistic staff. It does not publish any article, report, picture, etc. without the name and identity of its true creator.

● 3 *Jameah* uses abbreviations in identifying its domestic and foreign news sources. [...] The symbol [...] will be used to signal the omission of something which *Jameah* regrets it cannot publish for a variety of reasons, including shortage of space.

● 4 *Jameah* will, within the framework of its journalistic mission and to the best of its ability, reflect Iran's political, cultural and social geography by making social actions and reactions more transparent; it does not exempt any institution, group or phenomenon from this rule.

● 5 *Jameah* respects all the institutions, parties, associations and social groupings falling within the two – modern and traditional – sectors and strives to promote uplifting dialogue and discussion free of any bias or prejudice. *Jameah* hereby extends an official invitation to all institutions, parties and associations and all ethnic and cultural groupings – the official manifestoes of which include respect for the articles of the Constitution – to express their viewpoints on the country's overall concerns and current affairs in the special columns that *Jameah* will devote to them. Publishing these viewpoints is not tantamount to absolutely endorsing them; however, *Jameah* attaches value to and respects the presentation and juxtaposition of many viewpoints. These columns are henceforth at the disposal of social associations throughout the country. As far as *Jameah* is concerned, no group nor association should consider itself excluded from this possibility and opportunity.

● 6 *Jameah* will avoid using superfluous titles and honorifics for all state officials and will limit itself to their first names, surnames and area of responsibility. With respect to clergymen not holding any administrative and official posts, *Jameah* will use the accepted titles used in seminaries and, in the case of clergymen holding office, it will use their administrative titles. The leader of the Islamic Republic will be the only exception to this rule.

● 7 *Jameah* strives to bring specialisation to the different political, cultural and social arenas. To this end and in all its pages, it will reflect the views of specialists in various fields when reporting events or when raising issues of national importance.

● 8 *Jameah* intends to use methodical and scientific opinion polls in order to understand and reflect the fluctuations and developments in public opinion concerning important domestic and foreign events, and to put its services in this respect at the disposal of the nation and the government.

● 9 *Jameah* intends to pay particular attention to the well-known features of the press in the realms of analysis, reporting, using the language of images and caricatures, etc. taking a step towards putting Iran's press on a world-class footing.

● 10 *Jameah* will strive – by carefully scrutinising the performance of the country's official institutions [which are deemed to be answerable in accordance with the articles of the Constitution] and criticising social problems – to safeguard human rights and general freedoms, and to restore to "the fourth estate" – in its capacity as a civil institution – its role as a government guide and helper.

'*Jameah* believes these 10 principles can pave the way for change in the Iranian press. The newspaper's ultimate success hinges on the comprehension of the fact that the existence in Iran's Islamic society of a high-circulation, enthusiastic, lively, bold and critical paper that reflects the upheavals and changes in political and social geography, can also contribute to the stability of a strong political system and impede the penetration of those who greedily eye this sacred land.

'*Jameah* warmly shakes the hands of every single reader and is at the service of society with ever greater humility starting today.'

Editorial, *Jameah* 25 April 1998

Announcement jameah

Faraj Sarkoohi left for Germany last Wednesday. Sarkoohi first took part in a press conference in the city of Frankfurt and then accepted a cultural grant from the International Writers' Parliament.

Faraj Sarkoohi is to take part in the annual meeting of the Writers' Association [PEN] in Sweden. At the meeting, Sarkoohi is to receive the [Kurt Tucholski] prize that was awarded to him last year.

Sarkoohi has said he will return to Iran in two months and start working as the editor-in-chief of a cultural journal.

Our own correspondent, *Jameah,* **10 May 1998**

Journalists protest jameah

Forty-three of the country's journalists have signed a text calling on the commander of the Guards Corps to 'present a clear explanation of that part of his speech in which he threatened the press community, in order to do away with the anxiety felt by the country's journalists'.

The journalists said the remarks attributed to Rahim Safavi and published by the country's newspapers contain a threat against the country's press community. They add: 'Unfortunately, the statement issued by the Guards Corps' public relations office not only failed to remove the ambiguities contained in the remarks but, by repeating the accusations and threats against the country's newspapers, intensified the anxiety felt by the country's journalists.'

Our own correspondent, *Jameah,* **10 May 1998**

Say it with flowers jameah

In the wake of two attacks on the office of *Jameah* newspaper in Rasht and the letter from our editor-in-chief, along with a bouquet of flowers, to the assailants asking them to send their views to the newspaper's office in a written form for publication, a number of the *basijis* [volunteer force affiliated to the Islamic Revolution Guards Corps] of the town of Rasht have written to the editor-in-chief expressing surprise at his letter. In it they say; 'Our rejection of you is not tantamount to an acknowledgement of your publication.' The letter continues, 'The experience of the last two decades since the revolution

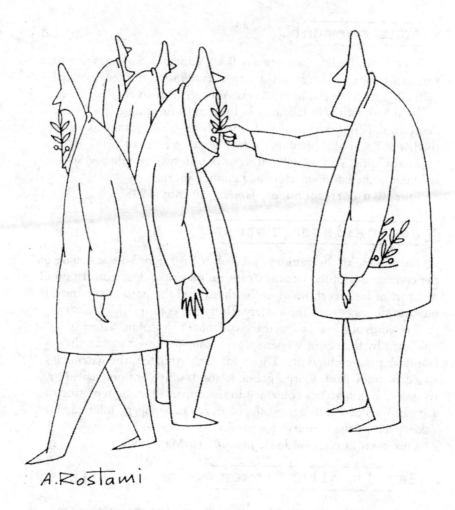

A. Rostami

teaches us that some people are incapable of engaging in rational
dialogue... What is your intention behind viciously attacking the
Guardian Council... Is the promotion of the Shamlus [Ahmad Shamlu,
Iranian poet, b. 1925] and Hedayats [Sadegh Hedayat, Iranian writer, d.
1951, author of *The Blind Owl*] who are famous, in thought and in
deed, for their theoretical and political corruption, not a blatant
indication of the West's cultural onslaught?'
Our own correspondent, *Jameah,* **10 May 1998**

Military government   jameah

Speaking at a meeting with naval commanders in April 1998, Islamic Revolution Guards Corps commander Rahim Safavi reportedly criticised some Iranian newspapers and spoke of 'cutting out tongues and severing throats' in this connection. He was said to have also condemned 'hypocrites disguised in clerical garb'.

Although the remarks attributed to the commander of the [Islamic Revolution Guards] Corps have not yet been confirmed by the commander's office, they have not been denied either. In view of the importance of the matter, it is essential to address their contents.

● 1 The intricacies of the thinking of the Corps commander and the question of what he considers to be in keeping with the revolution and Islam and what he does not, are unknown to us. Criticising his thinking is, therefore, not an option. Nonetheless, regardless of what his analysis is – whether it is true or false, whether it is correct or incorrect – it is essential to state that propagating any viewpoint by relying on weapons and armed troops is an absurdity and an impossibility. Even if superficial short-term gains are made, in reality and in the long term, such gains must be impossible by definition. If it were otherwise, in order to propagate their way of thinking, countries would simply expand their military forces instead of relying on writers, the press, clergymen, the media and so on.

Rationally, the endeavour would appear to be doomed because true thinkers would not allow their ideas to be propagated by the force of weapons and armed troops. Quite apart from anything else, such an attempt would be an insult to the thinkers. After swallowing everyone else, the said armed forces and troops would swallow the thinkers themselves or make them subservient; in which case, the thinkers would turn into armed troops and this would signal their end.

● 2 It would appear that the honourable commander of the Corps is not very familiar with the brother members of the Guards Corps. This must be why he can express so firmly on their behalf a view that is far from prevalent in the Corps. The results of the 2nd Khordad [23 May] election in one of the most important and largest centres of concentration of the honourable members of the Guards Corps have revealed that the average number of votes cast there for Mr Khatami was higher than the national average. There can be no doubt that the main message of 2nd Khordad was a rejection of violence and a rejection of the use of force and repression in solving problems. How is it possible then, with the presence of such wise people within the armed forces, to raise the possibility of taking measures which, even if initiated, would die in the womb.

● 3 Interference by the Corps in politics is not the same as the involvement of the armed forces in the country's domestic affairs. All the brothers in the Corps know that, in accordance with the will and testament of the Imam [Khomeini], they are forbidden from interfering in politics. Any interference by military men will not only not solve any problem for any individual or group, but it will, first and foremost, harm the effectiveness of the armed forces in the performance of their main task, which is the defence of the territorial integrity of the country.

In exactly the same way as the judiciary would also lose its effectiveness if it entered into politics.

The honourable commander of the Corps must realise that one cannot enter into the arena of politics carrying a weapon. The arena of politics has its own special characteristics. Using such phrases as cutting throats and... [sic] speaks of the total inexperience of the person using such expressions.

● 4 One of the most significant features of the said remarks is the insult directed at the clergy. It is unprecedented in Iran for a military man to speak with such insolence about the clergy. If you are a follower of the clergy and Islam, you have to accept that they are wiser and more capable of reforming society. This takes us back to the first point raised in this note: that is, you are ultimately asking the clergy to obey the bayonet.

'Political Commentary', *Salam*, **30 April 1998**

Always behind

jameah

MAS'UD BEHNUD

On the day Hasanali Mansur, the Shah's prime minister, was assassinated in February 1965, there was nothing about the incident in the two o'clock news bulletin that afternoon. That evening, the third item in the news was as follows: 'As the Iranian Prime Minister Hasanali Mansur was about to enter the parliament building today, he was wounded by a few bullets. The perpetrator of the crime has been arrested and the prime minister's condition is improving.'

When this item was broadcast, the prime minister had been dead for several hours. The people learned about his death much quicker than the Shah's intelligence, security and law enforcement forces, and were already seeking out the main cause. And, long before the radio announced – two days later – that the prime minister had died and Hoveida had been appointed prime minister, the people knew what was what. Even on this third day, the first item in the news was about how the Venezuelan ambassador had been granted an audience and submitted his credentials, and this was followed by a report about the Shah sending a greeting to the Queen of Holland on the anniversary of her ascension to the throne. Then they turned to Mansur's death and Hoveida's appointment as prime minister.

In those days, there were no satellite dishes, television news channels had not been established and the millions of small transistor radios, using just two little batteries, did not exist – as they do now – to enable people to inform themselves about the world. Today, all these things exist, but our radio and television are the same as ever, broadcasting the news about the President's letter and the leader's reply and, finally, the freeing of Gholamhoseyn Karbaschi one day after the event and at a time when the world's television channels and radio stations had broadcast the gist of the news 24 hours earlier and were, at that moment, carrying reports showing how the people were enthusiastically welcoming their popular mayor outside the prison and near his house.

During the 12 days Karbaschi spent in prison, international news networks – 'imperialism's news agents'! – broadcast accounts of this incident in all their news bulletins. It was a suitable occasion for Iranian radio and television to put their role of factional and clan mouthpiece behind them and to inform the people about what they wanted to know. But this did not happen. News imperialism won again and, once again, the conditions for this victory were brought about by Iranian radio and television themselves.

So, although in recent years it has become one of the manifestations of wisdom and prudence to blame domestic and foreign journalism which 'needlessly creates a commotion and is ill-intentioned' and to pull a blanket over the main cause with an 'on the one hand and then on the other' – as Mr Hashemi-Rafsanjani did in yesterday's Friday prayers – isn't it really time to seek the cause in our own graceless figures, who like to harp on the cultural invasion but who, in practice, pave the way [...] for that invasion?

Jameah, **18 April 1998**

Define security

resalat

AMIR REZA'I

The last few days have proved that the absence of the interior minister [Abdollah Nuri] was beneficial to the country's security. Not only did the provocative and disruptive behaviour of the real opponents of the rule of law not diminish on his return, they registered a noticeable increase.

It was this same interior minister who allowed a well-known group to hold a gathering and rally against the Guardian Council; who went straight from the airport [on his return from Saudi Arabia] to the house of an accused person by the name of Mr Karbaschi; and who, at this very moment, is engaged in breaking the law and showing blatant opposition to the law and the rule of law by forming 'the headquarters for supporting Karbaschi'! [...]

The judiciary has decided to put someone accused of embezzlement, bribery and misappropriation of public funds under temporary detention in keeping with the performance of its legal responsibilities. But, instead of supporting the implementation of justice, an interior minister, who claims to be the defender of the rule of law and the implementation of the law, opposes the process of the law and sets out to inflame the public and fan the flames of intrigue?!

What law, constitutional or otherwise, allows the honourable interior minister to interfere in the affairs of the judiciary? Has his eminence the minister completed all his other duties and dealt with all the country's problems falling under his jurisdiction so that he has the leisure to concern himself with the affairs of another legal body?

Mr Minister, are you aware that 780 village households were made homeless by the earthquake in Birjand? Are you aware that floods have caused damage in 95 villages in the Fereydun Shahr area? Are you aware that the village of Abkar, in Farsan, and all its residents have been buried underground? Is your first duty to establish headquarters to deal with these natural disasters or to establish a headquarters for supporting

Mr Karbaschi?! Are you not of the opinion that the formation of the headquarters for supporting Karbaschi is tantamount to cocking a snook at the law and the rule of law?! Is the headquarters not in reality a headquarters for supporting embezzlement, bribery and law breaking?! Why is it that you are fully committed to that part of your responsibilities that concerns the appointment and removal of governors-general, governors, district governors and even village heads – not even neglecting to support a mayor who has broken the law – but are not concerned about dealing with the problems encountered by people throughout the country, such as floods, earthquakes, etc?!

Mr Minister, what is the meaning – in terms of the rule of law – of the adoption, by you and your friends, of positions against the law?

It can be said decisively that not a shred of legal evidence or support can be found in the remarks made by the officials and [parliamentary] deputies who support Mr Karbaschi: one of them says 'he is from a clerical family', another that 'he has been a successful manager'; a third claims that 'this amounts to a virtual coup d'état' and a fourth that he has a splendid record; and so on.

What evidence or proof do you have to show that Mr Karbaschi has not engaged in embezzlement? Is everyone born into a clerical family or with a splendid past record immune to erring and mistakes?

Contrary to your claims that Mr Karbaschi's arrest was political, your angry reactions have shown that you are the one who is motivated by politics; the incident itself was merely a legal and juridical act.

Mr Nuri, you should put the investigation of one of your officials down to the judiciary's strength. That is to say, the judiciary must be strong and impartial enough not to make any distinction between a simple worker and the mayor of the state's capital. Where in all this do you see any indication that the judiciary has shortcomings?

This is nothing other than strength and justice.

Mr Minister, at a time when the eminent leader of the Islamic revolution [Khamene'i] has called on the heads of the three branches to consult on this case and asked that the results be made known to him, is your politicking and irrational, disruptive and partisan behaviour in the interests of the system, the country and the people?

Are you aware that all foreign radio stations and media, especially those of the system's number one enemies, such as Israel and America, have – just like you and your friends – not lost a moment in condemning the judiciary? What is the meaning of this uniformity, this unison? The main points in the reports, analyses and discussions on foreign radios have been as follows:

● The arrest of the mayor of Tehran is political and a manifestation of the struggle for power between the political groups ruling in Iran.

● The faction that lost the presidential election is taking revenge by arresting Karbaschi.

● The mayor of Tehran's arrest will lead to an unprecedented crisis in the Iranian state.

● The detention of the mayor of Tehran was a deliberate move to undermine Mr Khatami's government.

● The arrest of the mayor of Tehran will create a state of insecurity for the country's officials.

It is amazing that these same points form the main axes of the remarks made by the government spokesman, the eminent interior minister, the Office for Fostering Unity, the so-called 'Line of the Imam' coalition groups, and so on.

Mr Minister! Why have you got yourself into such a state at the thought of an investigation into the case of Mr Karbaschi? Why are you worried about him being tried in an open court so that justice is done?

Reconsider once again your angry and enraged assertion that you will not give an inch. Do you imagine you are waging war against infidels?!

Mr Minister, you say things without the slightest consideration, you interfere in the affairs of the other branches, you provoke tension, you are hell-bent on finding enemies, you put an offender on a pedestal and pour scorn on the executor of justice.

The Lord of the Faithful said to Malik Ashtar: 'Oh, Malik, keep a vigilant eye on the performance of your officials, lest the servant and the traitor turn into one and the same in your government.'

The judiciary is now engaged in a vigilant inspection and investigation.

Today, undermining the judiciary is to the benefit of counter-revolutionaries and the opponents of the system. Would the return of billions of tomans of plundered money to the government's coffers not be to the benefit of the government?

Excerpts from editorial, *Resalat*, 14 April 1998

Iran's 'perestroika' may be on thin ice – Credit: Blackburn/Rex

Karbaschi: four theories

jameah

SEYYED EBRAHIM NABAVI

Officials voice four essential theories on Karbaschi's arrest. The relationship between the people and officials in this dialogue varies.

First: officials understand what they're saying and the people understand what they're hearing. For example, that cases of embezzlement have to be dealt with and that the case of the mayor of Tehran is political.

Second: officials understand what they're saying but the people don't understand what they're hearing. For example, that it is essential that the mayor of Tehran not be allowed to have any visitors.

Third: officials don't understand what they're saying but the people understand what they're hearing. For example, that the mayor of Tehran helped Khatami in the election campaign and that this help is taken to mean embezzlement.

Fourth: officials don't understand what they're saying and the people don't understand what they're hearing. For example, that the country's second and third highest official have adopted a neutral silence in the case of the mayor.

Moral lesson: mutual understanding is a lovely thing.

Politico-moral lesson: the problem of many Third World states is that the people's intelligence quotient is higher than the intelligence quotient of officials.

'Fifth Column', *Jameah*, 12 April 1998

Hang him!

jameah

SEYYED EBRAHIM NABAVI

Let me draw your attention to some news which reaches us three months after the event.

This morning, Gholamhoseyn Karbaschi, the so-called former mayor of Tehran, took part in a news conference with *Sobh* [Morning] and *Farda Sobh* [Tomorrow Morning] [sarcastic reference to two anti-Karbaschi publications]. While confessing to the crimes listed below, he asked that he and all the other employees of Tehran Municipality be hanged for:

● 1 Attempting to overthrow the system of the Islamic Republic by building roads and motorways that could be used for transport purposes by the enemy.

● 2 Attempting to build high-rise buildings in order to allow the enemy to achieve the greatest possible mastery over sensitive points, especially in Guards and Africa Avenues.

● 3 Attempting to build hundreds of parks in various parts of Tehran to allow young people to have a wild time and to ease the distribution of drugs; and removing fences to facilitate the escape of drug dealers.

● 4 Attempting to provide financial assistance to committed brothers in order to corrupt them.

● 5 Attempting to stand in the path of the wind thus allowing large quantities of windfall gains to pass via him into the hands of the other faction.

● 6 Attempting to undermine the country's security by propagating luxurious living in Tehran and arousing considerable rancour by cleaning the city.

● 7 Attempting to build team houses for agents under the guise of cultural centres, which were, of course, captured by the revolutionary brothers.

● 8 Attempting to publish the so-called *Hamshahri* colour tabloid in order to degenerate public opinion and spread corruption and immorality by assisting so-called artists taking part in the Fajr Film Festival, and providing financial assistance to the festival.

● 9 Attempting to appoint the recently arrested and recently released district mayors and publishing falsehoods about their mistreatment and the existence of a prison for mayors; indeed, for attempting to do anything at all.

● 10 Arousing pain and sorrow among editors of newspapers belonging to the other faction and their families, such that, even after swallowing a variety of pills, their pain would still not go away.

● 11 Attempting to build a large number of park and ride facilities in order to waste the time of good Muslims.

● 12 Attempting to spy for the mayors of other cities by taking part in various conferences.

● 13 He also confessed that the 123bn tomans [US$400m] embezzlement, attributed to Fazel Khodadad and the brother of

Rafiqdust's brother, was, in fact, committed by him.

● 14 Attempted complicity to support President Mohammad Khatami and causing pain to the other faction by harping on about civil society.

Moral lesson: Justice must be done whether it involves the left-wing faction or the liberals or the Servants of Construction [now a political party], it's all the same [i.e. as long as it's any of the pro-Khatami groups, all is well.]

Well-known proverb: If you make your bed, you can make others lie on it.

'Fifth Column', *Jameah*, 5 April 1998

The road to Afghanistan   zanan

SHAHLA SHERKAT

This spring, a clause banning 'the exploitative use of women in images or contents; or humiliating or insulting the female sex; or encouraging adornments or embellishments; or creating conflict between men and women by resorting to a defence of its rights not based on legal and Islamic regulations' was added to Article Six, Chapter Four of the Press Law. It was an attempt to remove the problem known as 'women' from the pages of the Iranian press.

The proposers and defenders of the clause were the women members of the Women, Youth and Family Committee [in the *majlis*/parliament]. The opinion of one of them as expressed in the *majlis* is worth repeating: 'There has never been a proposal as progressive as this on women's issues.' For our part, we have never seen a knife slice off its own handle. Of course the deputies – who have been elected by the people – are free to give their opinion and vote as they please; just as the constituents are free to vote for the deputies of their choice in future elections. However, what these deputies should bear in mind is that their fate in the future depends on their actions in the present.

One thing is certain: combating the rule of law with regressive laws, preparing chain-like clauses against the ever-increasing dynamism of Iranian women and pulling them tighter every day is a cover for a more fundamental and long-term aim; namely, the crushing of freedom of expression. Both these measures are part of the wide-scale plan for revenge against a majority that expressed its 'No' couched in the form

Iran's women face an uncertain future – Credit: Ozer/Rex

of a 'Yes' [in the election of Khatami last year].

In confronting last year's unexpected phenomenon, it is natural that
the traditional school of thought should organise itself on a massive scale
to embark on the creation of economic, political and cultural obstacles.
Even more natural that it should focus part of its programme of
repression on women, who clearly played such a prominent role in
bringing about the national phenomenon. What seems less natural is
that the traditional school of thought is still failing to grasp that women
have – like it or not – entered the political arena and, as a result of their
participation, consider themselves stakeholders in political society. The
women of Iran will, therefore, remember the binding clauses that are
being chained to their arms and legs. They are no longer objects that
can be trotted out into the arena by different factions when the need
arises only to be locked up in their homes again when the need has
passed!

The said clause deals with two important issues concerning women:
first, the banning of insults against and the humiliation of women,
something that all men and women want. But reducing it to this clause
– especially on the basis of the interpretation favoured by the traditional
viewpoint – deflects the public eye from the constant and general
humiliation that is directed against women in our laws, culture, politics,
families and society. We will not list them exhaustively here.

The second – and seemingly the main purpose of the proposers – is
to ban 'creating conflict between men and women by resorting to a
defence of its rights not based on legal and Islamic regulations'. [Note
the pronoun 'its', normally used for objects, here refers to women;
note, also, that 'its' bans only the defence of the rights of women.]

In reality, the debates on civil and religious law that are being raised
in the Iranian press, especially in publications relating to women, are
aimed at doing away with conflict and discrimination between men and
women and, by drawing their attention to their silenced expectations,
making women aware of the obstacles this vacuum has created for them.
In fact, *majlis* deputies who have benefited from the social groundwork
laid out by the press and submitted bills to the *majlis* for the resolution
of the legal problems encountered by women, are among the consumers
of such publications. The proposal that dowries should be index-linked,
the reform of custody laws and so on are examples.

If we do not agree that this is the most effective clause the traditionalists could have come up with to halt moves by the press to inform women, the most optimistic reading of the situation is that some people have been so carried away by their slogans on the total health and security of society that they have been taken in by their own propaganda. A woman deputy attacked the press in a speech, saying: 'Why do you say the law has done nothing for children who are abused at home?' It might be of interest for you to know that, in its most recent ruling on this subject, a court was forced to ask for the father's permission in order to grant the custody of an abused child to its mother. [In Islam], the right of guardianship and custody belongs to the father; even when he kills a child the father incurs no punishment.

If the honourable women deputies believe the right to discuss and criticise religious and civil laws belongs to theologians and jurists alone, why is it that 'the honourable pious ones' and 'seminary circles' make no effort to discover the simple solutions that could rescue women from legal impasses?! They have already found ways round a number of taboos and given religious approval to, for instance, banks earning profit, the eating of sturgeon, playing chess and so on. In any case, the only way to deal with conflicts between men and women and to meet their needs is to allow discussion of religious and civil laws, not to stamp the seal of censorship on freedom of expression. It has been stated again and again that a need cannot be crushed by denial or excommunication. Demand will be satisfied one way or another. The winner is the one who seizes the market by supplying the right goods and satisfying the demand.

Another disturbing piece of news earlier this year was the approval of 'the general principles of the members' bill for bringing the administrative and technical affairs of medical institutions into line with the requirements of the shariah'. On the basis of this bill, 'the diagnosis, treatment and transport of patients must only be carried out by staff of the same gender and, in cases of need, staff of a different gender may be used on the decision of the highest-ranking official at the institution, in compliance with the requirements of the shariah and in the presence of a male relative of the patient'.

At one point, a taxi company, in an over-hasty decision, ordered its drivers not to allow women passengers to use the front seat. Thereafter, the army of exhausted women abandoned on street corners gradually threatened to turn into a swollen political tumour. [And the Prophet said: 'Those who go to extremes in religion will be defeated.'] If this ill-judged order had been complied with, who is to say that these tumours – compounded by dozens of other repressed demands – would not have burst open.

Now we have to watch as women turned away by hospital reception departments turn into political opposition groups. These women will put all this dogmatism down to religion, not to the regulations drawn up for them thanks to the inflexible minds of traditionalists. And spare a thought for how hard it is for women in this society to keep their faith. Is this discriminatory approach to women not tantamount to telling Iranian women to go and sit at home alongside Afghan women?

The interesting point is the punishment foreseen for anyone who offends against the contents of this bill: written warnings, fines, the closure of the institution. Everything has been taken into consideration except the life of the dying woman who has failed to get herself accompanied by a male relative. This bill goes so far as to go against theological treatises that – in accordance with the principle of 'safeguarding religion from blame' – have declared that women may be examined by male doctors under certain circumstances. The bill is apparently based on the decision that, in pursuit of political ends, it is even permissible to go beyond God's judgement since, in the words of the Quran itself we read, 'God wishes you comfort not suffering.'

Editorial, *Zanan*, March–April 1998. Shahla Sherkat is the managing director of *Zanan*

Religion versus democracy   jameah

ABDOLKARIM SORUSH

Religious societies must give priority to people's rights rather than their duties to the state. Only then will religion and democracy be compatible

[Many] are of the opinion that it is impossible to combine religion and politics successfully and that both will probably suffer as a result. They therefore hold that they should be kept in separate spheres and that we should not think about combining them. However, there are certain points that can, perhaps, help our judgement and shed light on the discussion.

First, you said that in a democracy, everything can be changed. We need to examine this. Political philosophers who have studied the matter say that although the possibility of change is very great in democracy it is not unlimited and absolute. That is to say, no democratic parliament in the world will issue a ruling that totally does away with people's rights, nor would it have the right to do so. In other words, the fact that people have rights is the fundamental principle of democracy; no democracy will go against this principle because it would destroy its own basis. Concepts of this kind, which are considered to be the foundations of democracy, are sacred within democracies; sacred, in the sense of being immutable and requiring preservation. But the essential point here is how to implement democracy in a religious society.

Religious people, who have voluntary accepted a set of boundaries, who have agreed not to change this or that law and who have consented not to touch a certain religious principle – why should they be unable to have a democratic state? Since what they have done, in the words of some scholars, is 'to refrain by will', they have consented not to do certain things by choice, not by force. Assuming the existence of a majority of religious people in a society and assuming that these religious people have themselves accepted not to transgress or violate certain religious laws or rulings, in such a society, some of the do's and don'ts of their society are by no means undemocratic.

Their society is democratic in the sense that the people have the right to choose their religion and to appoint and remove their rulers; to exercise collective participation as far as primary decisions are concerned; to play a role in changing those laws they consider alterable; to have a free press; to exercise a large measure of criticism, even with respect to such ideas as enjoining virtue and prohibiting vice; carry out the distribution of wealth, power and learning fairly; where religious understanding admits of plurality and the pluralistic aspects of religious sources are taken seriously. Such a society is very different from a dictatorial, closed society, in which one person, the ruler, has the last word in everything: what he says is the law and the people play no part in appointing or removing him. A society where there is no press freedom; where the only talk is of people's duties and they are not considered to have any rights; where power, wealth and learning are not fairly distributed; and so on.

However, the fact that 'people in that society do not tamper with some laws' is not because there is an external compulsion or obligation;

it is rather because of a choice they themselves have made internally. And, as long as they remain religious, they will be like this – unless they turn away from their religion.

I believe that the greatest emphasis in a religious society should be placed on people's rights. To the extent that people's rights are accepted in such a society and religious people are seriously committed to and abide by them, the way will be opened to religious democracy. The theoretical struggle to realise and establish a religious democratic state is intimately linked with the struggle we undertake to consolidate, understand and establish human rights. And the practical struggle consists of religious people engaging in the consolidation of a state. And, based on the fact that they are the majority, they make it incumbent on their state to respect their religious values; nothing more and nothing less. A dictatorial and aggressive understanding of religion is, of course, not compatible with democracy. But this is not the only kind of religious understanding. By altering it, the way will be paved for the compatibility of religion and democracy.

Excerpt from part IV of 'Roundtable on political freedom in Iran', *Jameah,* **21 April 1998**

Hearts cannot be won by force   iran

Political desk: Fereydoun Verdinezhad, the managing director of the Islamic Republic News Agency, has described what happened on 2nd Khordad [23 May 1997, the date of Khatami's election] as the making of an exceptional choice and the expression of a preference by the general public, a public who feels that many of its wishes are personified in the President.

Speaking at a ceremony marking the inauguration of a new IRNA building in the town of Shahrud yesterday, he said: 'We must all ask ourselves – in our capacity as the people involved in the country's cultural and news affairs if we have taken useful steps in the past year to pave the way for the realisation of Mr Khatami's aims and slogans or not?'

Continuing, he said: 'Mr Khatami and his cabinet have been subjected to more spoken and written criticism in less than a year than some governments throughout the length of their term.

'Attacking the government of Mr Khatami – in his capacity as the choice of 20 million people, a number that has doubtless grown considerably by now – as we approach the first anniversary of his election, cannot be deemed to be worthy.

'There is a danger that we will lose the climate resulting from the shining sun of the leadership and 2nd Khordad because we lack experience in and tolerance of freedom of expression.

'If what we voted for is to become a reality, Mr Khatami alone will not be able to achieve it; the strong link between the three elements of Islam, the leadership and national unity must continue to exist as in the other stages of the Islamic revolution and, wherever this link between Islam and republicanism is weakened, the rights of the nation, especially the rights of those who wield pens, will be endangered.

'Those who wield pens must pay a high price for defending the wish of the people and it will be a price worth paying.

'It is only possible to penetrate the hearts of your audience by winning their satisfaction and acceptance; if it were possible to achieve it by force, many of the world's strongmen would not lie buried beneath layers of history and, if it were possible to penetrate people's minds by force and impose ideas on them, our country today would be run by mindless strongmen.'

Excerpt from front-page report, *Iran*, 18 May 1998

Explanation   jameah

In the past few days, *Jameah* newspaper has been experiencing numerous problems, such as 'being scarce', 'being over-priced' and 'being available only in small numbers in the provinces'. In this connection, we would like to offer our readers the following explanations:

● The scarcity of *Jameah* is something that will continue to plague us until the problems arising from the shortage of paper and shortcomings in terms of printing and advertising are resolved. The provisional solution we have opted for is to print the eight inner pages of the paper in black and white; the savings made in this way will allow the newspaper to begin taking steps towards increasing the number of copies printed and preventing a price rise. At the moment, the resources have been made available for increasing the number of copies printed by 20,000 per day. And this number will increase to 50,000 in a short time. In this way, the newspaper's total circulation figure will reach 150,000 per day. By doing this, we hope to be able to respond to the market demand, while avoiding the need to increase the price of the newspaper.

● Unfortunately, reports suggest that, in some parts of the country, especially Tehran, *Jameah* is being sold to readers at higher prices than the official price of 40 tomans [US 12 cents]. In other parts, some newspaper tradesmen are holding the paper for their regular customers. *Jameah* announces that the price of the newspaper continues to be 40 tomans and it calls on newspaper kiosks not to engage in any kind of sharp practice. We also call on our honourable readers to report any such instances to the newspaper's distribution department [telephone numbers 652472 and 657974 only]

● *Jameah* will gradually increase the number of copies available for the provinces in parallel with the total number of copies printed.

Jameah would like to thank its readers for their expressions of sympathy and encouragement.

Jameah is thinking about the future.

Jameah, 12 April 1998

Sick intellectualism   resalat

'In Iran, intellectualism was born sick' – Ali Khamene'i, supreme leader, May 1998

Today is the anniversary of the decree issued by Mirza Shirazi, may he rest in peace, calling for a boycott of tobacco. Looking back at the tobacco uprising [1891] is beneficial for our society: on the one hand it lifts the veil from the intermediary role played by 'sick intellectualism', on the other it reveals in part the Shi'ite clergy's dedication, struggle against foreigners and love of the people and demonstrates religion's profound power in political movements.

On one side stands Mirza Malkum Khan, one of the founders of 'sick intellectualism', who, in exchange for £50,000, offered his country for sale to foreigners. Later, he was to obtain the lottery concession from the Shah and sell it to two British companies for £40,000. Later still, he established a publication by the name of *Qanun* [The Law] with the intention of propagating his western ideas and, in parallel with the publication, set up a freemasonry lodge.

On the other side stands the clergy who wanted to sever Britain's hand from Iran. Clergymen such as Mirza Mohammad Hassan Ashtiani, Sheikh Fazlollah Nuri, Haj Mirza Javad Tabrizi, Mr Najafi-Esfahani, Seyyed Ali Akbar Fal-Asiri, as well as the other clergymen of Tehran, Mashhad, Shiraz, Esfahan, Tabriz, Yazd and...and, at the head of them all, Mirza Shirazi, who defended the country's independence with selflessness, decisiveness and the support of the people.

In many countries, especially Third World countries, intellectualism is a positive force that, by relying on indigenous customs and traditions, tries to restore society's independence and identity in the face of foreigners... In Iran, however, intellectualism was born sick and, from the very first, set out to propagate irreligiosity and the worship of the West.

When Mirza Shirazi was writing openly to the Shah: 'Permitting foreigners to interfere in the internal affairs of the country explicitly violates the holy Quran, offends the government's independence, harms the country's order and causes anxiety to the peasants', Mirza Malkum Khan, the founder of sick intellectualism, was describing the clergy as the cause of the country's backwardness and, in a speech on Iranian civil consciousness, was expressing the following opinion: 'There can be no doubt that we must adopt the principles of European civilisation, but, instead of saying we have obtained them from London or Paris, or that it is being conveyed to us by this or that ambassador or government – which would not be accepted – it will be easier if we say that these principles arise out of Islam!'

A brief look at some of the characteristics of sick intellectualism will help identify this current more precisely in society as it stands today:

● The intensity of sick intellectualism's obsession with the West has made it lose its own self to the point that it obtains its measure of what is true or false, good or bad, right or wrong from the West and the western media.

● Because of its irreligiosity, sick intellectualism is congenitally anti-clergy. Although it prefers to achieve its aims by breaking the ranks of clergymen and setting them against each other, whenever it gains power, it has no qualms about dealing ruthlessly with the clergy. Mohammad Ali Khan Tarbiat, one of the recognised faces of sick intellectualism, was a member of the judicial court that sentenced Sheikh Fazlollah Nuri to death [in 1909]. When the clergy's ranks are broken, justice has sided with that section of the clergy that has not succumbed to sick intellectualism and has not ceased to combat it.

● Sick intellectualism is arrogant and impudent and demands that society and the people grant it the greatest respect, responsibility and resources.

● Sick intellectualism is not prepared to face danger. It, therefore, does not enter the field when people are encountering problems or in times of danger. For instance, in the opposition to the coup of 28th Mordad [19 August 1953], in the uprising of 15th Khordad [5th June 1963], in the coming into existence of the Islamic revolution [1979] and in its sacred defence [Iran-Iraq war], it is not alongside the people. But in periods of calm it finds conditions suitable for entering the field and, without feeling guilty about forsaking the nation in times of danger and with the utmost shamelessness, uses its impudent tongue to attack and bring into question all the nation's achievements and acts of selflessness. With great opportunism, it tries to reap where it has not sown and to benefit from the blood others have shed. And, since it sees the forces of the revolution as the greatest obstacle to this end, it tries to drive them away through character assassination. Look at the attempts at character assassination directed by the press at Sheikh Fazlollah Nuri during the constitutional period and the character assassination by some of today's sick newspapers directed at the Islamic revolution's devoted personalities, such as the commander of the Guards Corps.

● Sick intellectualism loves to talk and to wield a pen and, although it also has a presence in the arts, especially the non-native arts, its preferred terrain is that of books and the press and it uses sensationalism to bring every value into question. Look at the commotion made by *Jameah* and *Hamshahri* newspapers over the law banning the use of women's pictures for publicity purposes and the law on bringing medical affairs into line with the requirements of the shariah.

The main sphere of activity and recruitment for sick intellectualism is the academic environment and its intended target is young university students. Exploiting the relative ignorance of youth, it tries to deny its past and to present itself in a respectable light. Thus, the airing of a programme like *Hoviyat* [Identity] arouses its wrath [*Index 6/1996*]. This is why mass media have a duty to expose sick intellectualism's past record, as well as the acts of treachery committed by sick intellectuals. We must not allow this sickness to spread and upset the wise old man of the revolution any further.

Editorial, *Resalat*, 14 May 1998

The donkey who knew too much jameah

SEYYED EBRAHIM NABAVI

A young, superstitious man finds a donkey and takes it home with him. The man's brother-in-law is a computer engineer and he finds several computer discs in the leather collar around the donkey's neck. When he puts the discs in a computer he realises that certain operations have been carried out on the donkey that make it capable of recording nearby sights and sounds and capture them on computer discs; it is even capable of reading people's minds. Investigations reveal that the donkey has been working as an agent and spy for the Americans gathering information about Iranian society. When the donkey's secret has been uncovered and just as he is surrounded by security forces, the donkey is destroyed by remote control from an American satellite.

The above is a summary of the late night story broadcast as a radio play during the New Year holidays, under the title 'The donkey who knew too much', by Iranian radio [Voice of the Islamic Republic].

Political analysis: not only do the Americans use Iranian newspaper editors, artists, politicians, businessmen, foreign policy officials and others as spies, they have mobilised donkeys to serve the Pentagon and the CIA as well.

Brotherly warning: keep an eye on the donkeys; this invasion is not just a matter of one or two people or the occasional foray.

Security recommendation: a security committee, with the involvement of the Veterinary Association, the Agricultural Ministry, the Interior Ministry [independent of the current minister], the Foreign Ministry, Voice and Vision [Iranian radio and television], should be established to ensure that all enemy donkeys are exposed and destroyed, so that no trace remains of these mercenary CIA agents.

The Blind Owl: there are donkeys in life that gnaw away at and wound the human spirit like the plague.

Uncle Napoleon: the one thing that is without limit in humanity is its 'donkeyishness'.

Philosophical recommendation: to improve efficiency, we suggest that the head of Voice and Vision be appointed head of the Philosophy

Club and that another person – it makes no difference who – is appointed to head Voice and Vision.

From the regular satirical feature 'Fifth Column', *Jameah*, 23 April 1998

Full and frank discussions   jameah

SEYYED EBRAHIM NABAVI

A number of Tehran's district mayors – working under Tehran Mayor Gholamhoseyn Karbaschi – have been imprisoned during the past year. On being released, a few of them have said they were subjected to mistreatment, including lengthy periods in solitary confinement.

The newly-released mayors have taken part in a revelatory interview with our 'Fifth Column' correspondent and have spoken fully and frankly about what happened to them in detention. We have omitted the parts of the mayors' remarks that were unprintable. In the case of some of the mayors, who were not prepared to reveal their names, we have substituted the device [...] used by *Jameah* in such instances.

The mayor of district [...]: We were [...]. Then, we were taken to [...] with a few other people. And, for [...] days, we were [...] in a single room and, there, they did [...] to us and said [...]. We said [...]. And every day they did [...] and [...] to us. One day, they came and said, go. But, if you go out [...], otherwise [...]. As for us, we are now [...] but [...]. We are much better. Please don't print any of this.

Moral lesson: Wouldn't it be better to [...] so that, in Mr Karbaschi's case [...] and, to this end, [...] or [...]?

'Fifth Column', *Jameah*, 11 April 1998

All the world's a football payam-e emruz

When hundreds of Nahavandi women invaded the town's sports stadium in their desire to watch a football match, local officials and the town's Friday prayer leader found the solution to the problem by allowing them to do exactly that.

Speaking to *Payam-e Emruz* about the event, Fareq, one of Nahavand's physical education officials, said: 'The champion team of the student football league had been invited to Nahavand for a game. On the day of the match, about 2,000 of Nahavand's women invaded the pitch and settled in a part of the stadium that seats 15,000 people.'

Initially, officials and law enforcement forces had a mind to remove the women. However, since the stadium is vast and they were some distance from the men, they were allowed to stay and watch the match with the consent of the town's Friday prayer leader. No harm done.

Fareq went on to say: 'We wanted to prevent them because of the regulations laid down by the Physical Education Organisation. Permission has not yet been granted for women to be present as spectators at a match being played by men, although in one or two sports, women are allowed to be spectators. It was a good experience and fortunately nothing went wrong. However, given women's interest in football, the Federation should come up with a solution.

Earlier, in a similar incident, Tehrani women invaded Azadi Stadium in order to participate in the celebration ceremony marking the victorious return of the Iranian football team from Australia. And they managed to watch the ceremony.

News item, *Payam-e Emruz,* **May 1998**

Birth of a party   iran news

For the first time since the revolution Iran is allowing the formation of political parties

Latest reports indicate that with the advent of Hoseyn Marashi, a *majlis* deputy, Ali Hashemi, deputy managing director of the National Iranian Oil Company, as well as Fa'ezeh Hashemi, *majlis* deputy and editor-in-chief of the daily *Zan* [Woman], and with Gholamhoseyn Karabaschi as its secretary general, the six-member Servants of Construction, known as G6, has started its activities as a full-fledged political party. It is expected to officially announce its formation soon.

G6 was founded in 1375 [1996-97] on the eve of the fifth *majlis* elections, by Tehran's mayor, Gholamhoseyn Karbaschi, the then vice-president for parliamentary affairs Ata'ollah Mohajerani, governor of the Central Bank of Iran Mohsen Nourbaksh, vice-president for executive affairs Mohammad Hashemi, the then head of Iran's Atomic Energy Organisation Reza Amrollahi and the head of the Physical Training Organisation Mostafa Hashemi Taba.

The group, with its powerful management skills, played a major role in the fifth *majlis* elections as well as the 1997 presidential elections.

Despite being new in Iran's political structure, Servants of Construction [G6] rose rapidly in Iran's political arena. Its meteoric rise led some analysts to believe that, despite the resounding victory of Seyyed Mohammad Khatami in the presidential elections, his cabinet could be hijacked by this group.

The large number of G6 members in Khatami's Cabinet is an indication that those analysts were not far off the mark.

The reinstatement of Karbaschi and Mohammad Hashemi, and the occupation of the posts of the Ministry of Culture and Islamic Guidance, Central Bank of Iran and Physical Training Organisation by Mohajerani, Nourbakhsh and Hashemi Taba respectively, was the reward given to G6 for its endeavours during the presidential elections.

However, G6's joy was short-lived. After the temporary arrest of Karbaschi, an influential member of the group was confronted by a real challenge from its rivals.

Since four members of this group are related to the head of the Expediency Council, Ayatollah Hashemi-Rafsanjani, and the overall policies of the group are in line with those of the former President, it is said that he may exercise too much influence over the group. However, Hashemi-Rafsanjani has always been reluctant to identify himself with any particular political group or line of thought.

In this context – and in view of the verbal attack of the deputy for Damavand, Ahmad Rasouli-Nezhad, on Rafsanjani and the subsequent silence of the rightists vis-à-vis this issue – it is possible that Hashemi is no longer interested in keeping a close relationship with the rightists and is trying to invest all his political capital in a unified political party.

Meanwhile, it is said that Karbaschi will go on trial soon, so his position as the secretary general of the Servants of Construction Party will enhance his power, enabling him to deal with his detractors with the full support of his party, as was the case with the former Mayor of Paris and current French President, Jacques Chirac.

Minister of Culture Ata'ollah Mohajerani, in his interview with the *Los Angeles Times* welcomed the upcoming trial of Karbaschi, saying: 'We are confident that no court can level any charges against the mayor.' This is indicative of the fact that the Servants of Construction are ready with a full hand to face the serious challenge of the Karbaschi trial.

Editorial, *Iran News*, 20 May 1998 ❏

FA'EZEH HASHEMI

What every woman wants

An interview with the founder and managing editor of Iran's latest paper, *Zan*, the first daily for women

Women's problems have been exposed and discussed all over the world over the past decade; we felt it was time we moved along in the same direction. And given that one of the missions of the press is to inform people and raise the level of society's understanding, it became imperative to have a paper devoted to women.

The country's press as it exists at present pays only scant attention to the difficulties and problems of women or to their positive achievements and abilities. The problems that have been raised so far in relation to women are only part of the reality. In the light of my own experience, I felt there was a huge vacuum on women's issues in the country's publications; I started Zan (Woman) to fill this gap.

We aim to discuss the full range of women's issues, including the legal, political, social and cultural. As well offering information and practical guidelines to our readers, the paper will act as a forum for women to discuss their problems and difficulties. We shall also cover social, political, cultural and sporting issues from other parts of the world.

Alongside our focus on women's affairs, we shall, like any other paper, cover issues related to Iran and the world in the best way possible. Let me be clear: contrary to what many people think, Zan is not a 'woman only' daily; men should read it to raise their awareness of women's problems. Since the majority of decision makers in our country are men, this would undoubtedly affect their decisions.

[Iran] has a limited number of publications concerned with women's issues; this does not reflect the advances that have been made by our women in different arenas. I'm not saying they are full of holes that we can fill, but since most of them are weeklies or monthlies, they have less opportunity to look at these issues. There is a need for a daily devoted to women's issues alongside existing publications.

I do not see any problems that are specific to the women of our society: the problems women face today are common to women all over the world. The most important problem is patriarchal attitudes; these have governed people's minds globally for centuries. Women are unlikely to be valued as long as such attitudes persist. For instance, that men should be the boss inside and outside the home and that women should simply obey them.

Unfortunately, patriarchal attitudes are not confined to men; women within the family and in their role as mothers discriminate between their sons and their daughters. They place the responsibility for running the household on the shoulders of the girls and let the boys off duties which are often their sole concern. The humiliations inflicted on girls within the family destroy the spirit of shared labour within the family and lead to discrimination and inequalities between men and women.

Above all, women in our society lack representation in key positions – both in the decision-making and executive sectors – and women and men are unequal before the law.

Ultimately, women make men responsible for decisions affecting them and this creates problems. For instance, by and large, the law is adequate and comprehensive but the problems are created by it being implemented by men. These problems will be largely resolved when women are in a position to formulate laws and, more important, when they are actively involved in implementing them. For instance, with the revival of the Family Court [established 1968/69] and the presence of women legal advisors during its proceedings, when male judges have to take the advice of the women advisors into account, many of the present shortcomings will be remedied.

Apart from the family environment, women complain of discrimination in the workplace; appointments and selections are made on the basis of gender rather than ability. Such discrimination is not unique to our society. Men in most places enjoy better educational, employment and earning opportunities. ... We need educational development to bring about changes. *Zan* will support and promote such changes, offering practical solutions by experienced and qualified people within the context of prevailing conditions in our society.

Political participation does not merely mean casting one's vote. Women will participate actively in politics when they succeed in occupying political posts. After the revolution, women made impressive advances in the sciences but this is not reflected by their presence in the higher echelons of places like the universities and government departments where they are noticeably lacking. There is only one woman in the cabinet [vice-president and head of the Environmental Protection Organisation Ma'sumeh Ebtekar].

To some extent women have themselves to blame. When women keep away from public life and do not participate in social issues, they are clearly circumscribing their own strengths and abilities. Women must develop their knowledge and skills and play an active role in the public arena. Then they will become more aware of their rights and be able to defend them.

Feminism is about defending women's rights, not, as some seem to think, about the replacement of patriarchy by matriarchy. Again, there are some who associate feminism with the wanton and unrestrained behaviour of western women. This is not my understanding of the term. We are not after the domination of men by women; nor, God forbid, do we want unfettered and limitless freedom. What we say is that women should participate on an equal basis – legal and social equality without reference to gender. We shall give space to those aspects of women's social rights which have by and large been ignored until now. We do not seek special privileges just because we are female; but nor, simply because we are female, do we want to be deprived of our just rights. ❏

Excerpt from an interview in Hamshahri, *31 May 1998, on the launch day of* Zan. *Interview by* **Banafsheh Purnaji**. *Translated by Florida Safiri*

EDWARD LUCIE-SMITH

Kingdom of the middlemen

I had never been to Hong Kong before the handover, so have no impressions to offer about what the atmosphere there was like before the event – now just a year ago. One thing, however, I did immediately notice, which was that people had little interest in talking about the handover itself. When I asked one educated Hong Kong Chinese what his impression of the various ceremonies had been, he paused briefly, then said: 'Oh, we all thought they had very little to do with us. They were something for the British and the mainland Chinese. If we watched things at all, we stayed home and watched them on television.'

Any attempt at deeper probing was politely resisted, both by Chinese acquaintances and also, to some extent at least, by expatriate Britons and Americans – especially those who have already lived in Hong Kong for a long time. The present political condition of Hong Kong and, directly dependent on this, the future of free speech in Hong Kong, are not things that anyone really wants to discuss at length. Two things, however, are noticeable. One is that Christopher Patten's reputation does not stand particularly high among the members of the expatriate community. I heard him several times accused of having had a very imperfect understanding of the economic needs and future of the city. The other is that the leaders of the 'democratic' movement, in particular the high-profile politician Emily Lau, were given a surprisingly rough ride in the local English-language press. Despite this, it was the 'democratic' group that triumphed in recent local elections, though voters knew that, because of the controls imposed by China, they were doing no more than vote for the members of a licenced opposition.

Given the nature of the situation, one has to look at other indicators.

The future of free speech in Hong Kong is undoubtedly closely linked to the development, or lack of it, of Hong Kong's economy. The general feeling was that the British were handing over an economic jewel – a financial mechanism so successful and so finely tuned that the mainland Chinese government would be foolish to interfere with its functioning. But would it be able to resist tinkering, on ideological grounds, with the 'special economic zone' within China that Hong Kong was now to become?

Things don't look quite so simple today, least of all from within Hong Kong itself. One reason is the general meltdown that has taken place in Far Eastern financial markets in the course of the last six months. All the so-called 'tiger economies' are sick. As I write, there is constant speculation, despite vehement denials, that the Chinese government may be about to devalue, and this diary may well be overtaken by events. Hong Kong has resisted the downturn better than more vulnerable economies, such as Indonesia, Malaysia and Korea, but there is still a great deal of anxiety. A particular cause for concern is high negative equity in the Hong Kong property market which, during the 1990s, rose to unprecedented heights. A lot of people bought supposedly prime property with borrowed money, and now it is worth substantially less than they paid for it. People with a negative-equity problem have less stake in the place. This remark applies with especial force to the wealthy Hong Kong Chinese elite, who have already diversified their interests, and who have large holdings elsewhere in the world. If they were to bale out, the political future of Hong Kong would look very different, as in political terms they form a kind of third force, situated between the westernising 'democrats' on the one hand, and the mainland Chinese government on the other.

When one begins to look at the actual detail of life in present-day Hong Kong, other factors begin to appear. Those who identify themselves with Hong Kong, as a place with a separate and special future, focus their fears, not on the mainland in toto, as the Leviathan which may swallow their city whole, nor on Beijing, as the symbol of communist government, but on Shanghai. Shanghai is the economic powerhouse of the new China. If labour is cheap in Hong Kong, it is cheaper still in and around Shanghai. That city is the place where vast new fortunes have been made, often in an atmosphere of political and economic skulduggery reminiscent of the chaotic, violent China of the

1920s and 1930s. The current rulers of mainland China have close links to Shanghai, closer, in terms of birth and sentiment, than their links to Beijing. The corruption and gangsterism which flourish sporadically in present-day China manifest themselves in Shanghai, and have begun to take on a high profile elsewhere, especially in Macau, now on the eve of its own handover to the Chinese. Macau is suffering from a serious security problem, with frequent gangland killings. These killings are linked to a struggle for control of the lucrative local gambling industry, and elements of the Red Chinese army are said to be implicated.

Another, perhaps surprising, factor as a generator of unease is the new Hong Kong airport, due to open in July 1998. The old airport Kai-Tak has long been considered inadequate and indeed dangerous, unsuited both to today's very large aircraft and to the amount of traffic it was expected to carry. The mainland Chinese authorities obstructed the building of a new facility during the run-up to the handover, as a way of putting pressure on the British authorities. At the same time, there was friction between governor Patten and the locals over the financing of the rapid-transit system which the new airport required. Now this airport is actually functional it is likely to bring changes which were, perhaps, unforeseen.

There will, of course, be even more flights to Hong Kong. Cathay Pacific, the Hong Kong-based airline, has already announced a major increase in traffic from the UK. But the local perspective will change. Hong Kong was almost the last remaining large city with a major international airport within the boundaries of its urban area. Where these airports survive elsewhere, as Santos Dumont does, for example, within Rio de Janeiro, they have all been turned over to local traffic. Till the end of June, it was possible to travel out of Hong Kong almost on impulse. This was especially true of travel to Taipei, and it is one of the reasons why the bonds, business and personal, between Hong Kong and Taiwan have remained so strong. The new airport may, in a general sense, make it even easier to get to Hong Kong than it is now, but at the same time it will subtly loosen some important links. In particular, it will have a levelling effect: Hong Kong will become just one more big Chinese city, one more major Asian city where there is a major slog between the airport and your place of business, or, in the case of visitors, between the airport and their hotel.

In addition to the airport, two other features of present-day Hong

Credit: Rex

Kong deserve a contemplative look from anyone trying to predict the
future of the UK's ex-colony. Neither has gone unremarked by visitors,
but neither has played much of a role in the calculations of political
pundits. One is the flourishing Hong Kong antiques trade, with its
centre in Hollywood Road. The other is the Filipinas.

The small store-fronts of Hollywood Road, and the large building
close to it which offers three floors of small antique-shops are a truly
astonishing sight. It's not unusual to see a shop window crowded with at
least 20 Neolithic burial urns, or to enter a booth and find the Tang
horses lined up in rows – a dozen large, a dozen medium-sized and a
dozen small. There are so many of these antiquities, and so little

concealment about the sheer quantity available, that one can assume, I think, that the vast majority are genuine – this despite the legendary prowess of the Chinese as forgers of art. The sources for these objects are illegal excavations throughout mainland China, often linked to the great projects currently going forward there, such as the damming of the Yangtze River. The geographical spread covers the whole of Chinese territory – there are quite numerous so-called 'Sino-Siberian' objects from sites in Mongolia, for example. The time-span is more restricted: it ranges from the Neolithic to Sung. There is not much that is later than about 1200AD. – no polychrome porcelains or flashy jades of the kind beloved by rich Hong Kong Chinese collectors. In a word, all this stuff comes from graves.

I think one can deduce several things from this spectacle. It serves as a reminder of the age-old wealth but also of the age-old self-sufficiency of Chinese culture. Hong Kong is going to find it hard to resist that pull. It also serves as a reminder of the elaborate clandestine organisation needed to keep these objects flowing into Hong Kong. Many middlemen play their part in bringing those Sino-Siberian bronze plaques from China's remote northern borders to this entrepôt in the south. And every one of the transactions has been 'unofficial'. It is not only the Macau gambling that breeds gangsterism – it is the antiquity trade as well. Every deal strengthens the bonds between Hong Kong as a social organism and the more worrying aspects of the new China

Every Sunday – their one day off – the young Filipina maids and nannies meet in Hong Kong's otherwise deserted business district. They spread their picnics under the pillars that support Norman Foster's glittering glass tower, built as an expression of faith in Hong Kong's future. They twitter and gossip and do each other's hair. There are hundreds, if not thousands of them. The spectacle is so charming that it takes an effort to remember that these are people without rights, brought here by terrible economic necessity. Even if the Hong Kong democrats succeeded in converting Hong Kong's new masters to their point of view, it would not be democracy for everybody in what is now called the 'Special Economic Zone'. Very far from that. ❏

Edward Lucie–Smith is a well known art critic and author. He is currently collaborating with Judy Chicago on Images of women in art *to be published next year.*

BARRIE LAW

Appleby Horse Fair

Ever since its establishment in 1685 the Appleby Fair has attracted Roma horse traders. Now it is the last great Gypsy gathering in England

Showing horses to prospective buyers – 1950s

Romany campfire – 1961

Cooling horse and rider – 1990s

Gallows Hill – 1943

Putting horse
through its paces –
date unknown

Appleby town centre – 1902

The River Eden – 1990s

Barrie Law is a photographer and archivist. He has published several books on Travelling people and the Appleby Fair.

GRANVILLE WILLIAMS

Digital dystopia

What will it mean for free expression when the box in the corner can supply rolling newsbites, hard-core, the weekly shopping and the National Curriculum?

There's a burgeoning literature predicting a new electronic information and leisure age. It's a vision based on the superfluity of channels soon to be on offer through the imminent digital revolution. Proponents of this vision have a good deal of evidence to support their case. In 1983 17 west European countries possessed between them 36 public channels and only a small number of private commercial channels, including Britain's strictly regulated ITV. Ten years later the number of public channels had hardly increased, but over 100 new commercial cable and satellite channels had been launched, many of them new 'thematic' channels dedicated to sports, music, news, etc.

If these channels represented the first wave of new media, with some disappearing and others establishing themselves and becoming very profitable (for example, Rupert Murdoch's UK satellite system, BSkyB) alongside the traditional structures of broadcasting, the argument runs that the second wave of new media made possible by digital terrestrial and satellite television will deepen and extend access and diversity because broadcasting will begin to resemble publishing.

Hamish McRae, writing in the *Independent* presented his view about the 'seismic change' which will hit the industry, where 'quite quickly we will go not just to several hundred channels but perhaps to a couple of thousand channels'. Instead of television being driven by producers who decide what the public should watch, the industry will become consumer driven: 'Think of the magazine rack at W H Smith: strings of titles covering everything from scuba diving to soft porn. Though the bulk of the sales are still dominated by a few dozen long-established

titles, it is relatively cheap to launch a magazine. Any company with
£250,000 or so can have a crack at starting a nationally distributed
monthly. That means an entrant can suddenly hit upon something new
that attracts the consumers'.

For over five years the business and media press has been predicting
and promoting a similar vision of the new multimedia age. Television,
moving on from its limited terrestrial and satellite channels transmitted
through the old analogue technology, will be transformed into a two-
way medium offering an abundance of information: movies-on-demand,
video games, educational programmes, niche channels from Playboy or
science fiction, home shopping, telebanking, teleconferencing,
teleworking, and so on. The European Publishers Council, which
lobbies across the European Union on behalf of a broad range of media
groups, predicts a 'proliferation of media outlets, greater consumer
choice and control over what they see, hear and read and the ability to
interact with the media'.

The technological advances underpinning these predictions are
becoming familiar to a wider public: new digital satellite and terrestrial
systems, fibre-optic cables, and the growth of the Net. When Astra
launched in 1995 the first of four satellites with 56 digital transponders
between them, Europe's leading commercial media concerns rushed to
book space (BSkyB booked 11). SES, the company operating the Astra
satellites, claims each of its satellites' transponders will be capable of
broadcasting five to 10 television channels. Digital compression also
means that television signals can be carried on telephonic cable, and
cable companies and telecommunication operators are now beginning to
promote new channels and services. Placed alongside the phenomenal
growth on the internet, these technologies, it is argued, make redundant
old issues and concerns about regulation or media concentration
threatening diversity and pluralism. We are entering an era of
information choice and profusion.

The evidence and assumptions behind this view are shared by
influential political groupings. At the European level, an important
Green Paper on Convergence (January 1998) endorses it; in the United
States the Advisory Council on the National Information Superstructure
produced a glowing report, A Nation of Opportunity; and in the UK
the Culture, Media and Sport Select Committee, chaired by senior
Labour MP, Gerald Kaufman, produced a report entitled The Multi-

Media Revolution which recommends the creation of a separate
Department of Communications to hasten its arrival.

'inadequately funded schools will find themselves forced to divert resources from the classroom to cyberspace'

But there are a number of questions and concerns about this vision of the digital future. The analysis of it is driven and shaped by narrow technological criteria and assumptions, and it's the pervasive technological determinism which is worrying. One of the most astute commentators on this issue is Brian Winston, whose recent book *Media Technology and Society* traces the historical development of electrical and electronic systems of communication. His book, 'an anti-technicist polemic', argues that social, political, cultural and economic factors are the prime determinants of technological change.

But policy-makers at the moment seem transfixed by the predicted marvels and transformations which the information revolution heralds, and policy which has emerged takes a narrow focus, rather than considering the broader picture. One area where this is happening is in schools. In the USA, Vice-President Al Gore's enthusiasm for the information superhighway has led to a major emphasis on wiring up schools so that children can study and access information through the Net. It's a policy which has been enthusiastically adopted in the UK by the Labour government through the concept of a National Grid for Learning.

In 1922 Thomas Edison predicted that 'the motion picture is destined to revolutionise our educational system and...in a few years will supplant largely, if not entirely, the use of textbooks.' Fast forward to 1997 and President Clinton campaigns for 'a bridge to the 21st century...where computers are as much a part of the classroom as blackboards.' It's an enthusiasm which will cost $40 billion to $100 billion over five years, but to realise it school budgets for music, art, physical education, and library books are being cut. Schools have embraced successive rounds of new technology, where big promises for improvement in teaching and learning are made by the technology developers' research, but are not realised. Clifford Stoll, author of *Silicon Snake Oil: Second Thoughts on the Information Highway* recalls his school days from the 1960s: 'Computers in classrooms are the filmstrips of the 1990s. We loved them because we didn't have to think for an hour; teachers loved them because they didn't have to teach; and parents loved them because it showed their schools were high-tech. But no learning happened.'

Another cause for concern is the growing commercialisation of an area of society hitherto relatively free from such pressures. Education has become a priority area of activity; in the United States there is an active corporate marketing presence in every school, with companies such as the cable giant TCI and Walt Disney, moving into the production of educational material. The UK government's plans for a national data grid will create the same situation. It sets out a programme for persuading schools to pay for 'competing managed services' – government approved consortia of hardware suppliers, service providers and content creators. No wonder Bill Gates on a flying visit to the UK endorsed the Labour government scheme to put every school on the internet. This is exactly where he sees Microsoft's future market. In spite of some difficulties with the US Justice Department, the company is committed to developing its internet Explorer as the universal front-end for accessing internet content – much of it already owned by Microsoft, or its commercial allies. It's also why the powerful UK-based telecommunications company, BT, has become actively involved in working with the government on building school links to the internet.

The classroom is being prised open as a free-for-all for business interests, whereas it should be a space where students acquire information and skills independent of corporate pressures. The danger with the UK and US government plans is that inadequately funded schools will find themselves forced to divert resources from the classroom to cyberspace. Schools without the internet will be perceived as unattractive choices, and the offer of 'seed-corn funding', free connection and generous discounts from hardware, software and service providers will be irresistible. Once on the technology treadmill, schools will have to spend more and more to deliver the services students expect. This could push the focus of education away from the processes of reading, thinking, and listening taking place in individual schools towards a costly, but dubious, nostrum.

In broader media policy terms, the identical fascination with the technical possibilities associated with digital systems is worrying. The European Union Green Paper on Convergence states very baldly that 'digital technology allows a substantially higher capacity of traditional and new services to be transported over the same networks and to use

Rupert Murdoch and friend – Credit: Rex

integrated consumer devices for purposes such as telephony, television and personal computing'. Because the technology is converging, it argues, there has to be the 'right regulatory framework in order to maximise the benefits of this in terms of job creation, growth, consumer choice, cultural diversity'. It is this emphasis which is worrying politicians such as Labour MEP, Carole Tongue.

She believes there 'will be no sudden bolt of lightning which will hook every one of us to the panoply of services that are imaginable, if not currently available. Technological convergence will be an evolutionary process. New media forms will not displace television. They will complement it'. She opposes the powerful telecom lobby which argues for reduced regulation by saying that, because a fax and a film can be transmitted and received in the same way, they should be regulated in the same way. Implicit in this approach is the belief that the explosion in the number of TV channels means there is no longer any need for public service broadcasting, because the new services will deliver every programme that we could ever wish for. 'The kind of market-led, fragmented free-for-all envisaged by the Green Paper is inimical to public service requirements,' she argues.

Some other facts support Tongue's analysis. According to Independent Television Commission figures for 1997, it was possible to receive 89 channels in the UK, but 34 of these got a total viewing share of 0.01%, and there was some rounding up by the ITC to get to that figure, whilst the (then) four terrestrial channels took between 62 and 65% of terrestrial viewing. Even in the US, with the highest rate of internet usage and a much more developed cable network service, the four largest TV networks retained a market share of 61% in 1997.

And what will be on the new digital channels? The *Independent's* Hamish McCrae used the W H Smith analogy which is telling, because the company plays a key role in determining what printed products do and don't get onto British shelves. Indeed, early in 1996 the company, against a background of poor profits, decided to pull some 350-400 low circulation and low-revenue magazines from its shelves, leading to the subsequent failure of some titles. What is absent from all the alluring visions of the multimedia age is the key role of the distributor, or 'gatekeeper', determining what does and doesn't get onto the channels. This depends crucially on ownership, and whilst the hype suggest there will be bandwidth for every kind of channel brought into existence, the reality is, and will remain, different.

Cable TV in the US was presented to the public as a new communications technology that would break the monopoly of the big three TV networks and provide dozens of new channels, representing diverse interests and viewpoints. An excellent issue of the US media magazine *Extra!* pointed out: 'We've got dozens of channels, all right, but most of them are owned by an interlocking set of a half-dozen or so giant corporations.' The major cable system operators and programmers are in fact business partners with their supposed competitors, and it's almost impossible to get a new channel carried on major cable systems without offering a piece of the action. An analysis of the major players who want to move into digital broadcasting reveals that there aren't any new entrants – the start-up costs are too high – but rather alliances and joint ventures of existing media, IT and telecommunications groups.

And what about the programmes, and the range and quality on offer, on the new channels? The first and obvious point is they will be paid for, either by subscription or pay-per-view, and therefore operate according to commercial criteria. It will mean going for what the industry inelegantly calls 'killer applications' – movies-on-demand, sports, games, music, home shopping, 'adult movies' and so on. In addition, many of the channels will be automated to unspool mindlessly 24 hours of programming, uninterrupted by bulletins about national or global events. The opposite, in fact, of interactivity. And more generally, the dominance of corporate, rather than public service values, and the avoidance of clashes of corporate interest, will lead to bland, uncontroversial programming, a form of silent commercial censorship.

A dramatic example of this occurred when Walt Disney took over the US TV network, ABC. A US$12 billion outstanding lawsuit against an ABC investigative programme by the tobacco and food giant Philip Morris was hurriedly settled, even though the journalists involved refused to be part of the climbdown because they believed the programme was indisputably accurate.

So will we, the consumers, be rushing out to buy the new black boxes so we can immerse ourselves in these digital services? Ask your kids. ❏

Granville Williams edits Free Press *for the Campaign for Press and Broadcasting Freedom, and teaches Journalism and Media Policy at the University of Huddersfield.*

Roma/Gypsies:
A European Minority

Jean-Pierre Liégeois
and Nicolae Gheorghe

Minority Rights Group
International
Report

MRG's Report provides a new analysis of Roma and their history. It explains the complexity of Roma identity and discusses the changing and evolving nature of Roma communities. Significantly, it details Roma efforts at organization and political action.

A4, 36pp, £4.95/US$8.95. Updated January 1998.

Available from MRG:
tel +44 (0) 171 978 9498; fax +44 (0) 171 738 6265.
e-mail: minority.rights@mrg.sprint.com
website: www.minorityrights.org

Photo: Marc Schlossman

SUPPORT FOR INDEX

Index on Censorship and the *Writers and Scholars Educational Trust (WSET)* were founded to protect and promote freedom of expression. The work of maintaining and extending freedoms never stops. Freedom of expression is not self-perpetuating but has to be maintained by constant vigilance.

The work of *Index* and *WSET* is only made possible thanks to the generosity and support of our many friends and subscribers world-wide. We depend on donations to guarantee our independence; to fund research and to support projects which promote free expression.

The Trustees and Directors would like to thank the many individuals and organisations who support *Index* and *WSET*, including:

If you would like more information about *Index on Censorship* or would like to support our work, please contact Dawn Rotheram, Director of Development, on (44) 171 278 2313 or e-mail dawn@indexoncensorship.org